Reviews for Nikki's first book

Housesitting in Australia

*Nikki has written not only an inspiring book about how to transform your life, but also a practical and information rich guide to house sitting. This is a must read for anyone searching for a bit of adventure in their lives and who would like to try house sitting as a way to travel on a budget!*

Kylie Fuad

Director

www.AussieHouseSitters.com.au

*Nikki Ah Wong gets it! Her book demonstrates, once again, that living life on our own terms is the best way to find the satisfaction that we all seek. House sitting is one way to support a dream. Whatever your dream might be, when people like Nikki tell their personal stories of triumph, it empowers us all.*

Teresa Roberts author of 'Finding the Gypsy in Me    -Tales of an International House Sitter'

www.findingthegypsyinme.com

# Is the Davi*T*

# Supposed to Fall Off?

*A First Time Sailor in a Wild New Zealand Sea*

## Nikki Lentfer

(Previously writing as Nikki Ah Wong)

Also by Nikki Ah Wong

*Housesitting in Australia: Big Adventure on a Tiny Budget*

*A Middle-Aged Princess in Tramping Boots: Adventures in life, love, and house-sitting*

*Junk Mail Princess: Adventures in Life, Love, Renovation, and Junk Mail*

*The House Sitters Companion: Journal and Planner*

Copyright © 2015 Nikki Ah Wong

2023 Edition

All rights reserved

ISBN-13: 978-0-9872553-4-1

ISBN-10: 0987255347

*Twenty years from now you will be more disappointed by the things you didn't do than by the ones you did do. So, throw off the bowlines. Sail away from the safe harbor. Catch the trade winds in your sails. Explore. Dream. Discover.*

*H. Jackson Brown, Jr.*

# Contents

# Preface

You know those days when the clock seems to crawl and the end of the day is unsatisfying? My sailing trip was the opposite of that. It was a time to feel alive, to be outrageously challenged and completely out of my comfort zone.

Sometimes I was tired, or bored, or sore, but mostly I was outrageously happy. There is nothing like a spot of imminent danger to bring life into brilliant colour.

Sailing was Phil's dream and I was towed along in his excited wake. When my husband Phil said 'Let's go sailing' it sounded relaxing, much like 'let's go for an afternoon nap'. I thought sailing would be mostly days running effortlessly with the wind while Phil and I stood sedately on deck, watching the world go by and sipping cool drinks.

When I got back ashore, I looked up sailing in the dictionary. It is defined as 'to move, float or glide smoothly through water or air'. My first experience of sailing was less like the dictionary definition of sailing and more like bungee jumping with dolphins, or pogo jumping with occasional sightseeing stops along the way.

My sailing experience was not typical. If you are reading this and considering whether sailing is for you, do not let my experience put you off. Plenty of people love it out on the ocean and do find it relaxing. Many days for us were very dramatic, and sailing isn't always like that, I promise.

When we took our trip, we forced our passage. That is, we went when it was not ideal conditions because we needed to be north in a few weeks. That meant rough seas and a bumpy trip, at least until we reached protected waters.

It was a hard start for me, but it got us to some interesting coastal towns. We visited a French Catholic Mission house built in Russell, explored the historic Waitangi Treaty Grounds where New Zealand's founding document was written and signed, and discovered many beautiful islands and interesting towns around the coast.

It was a bit like a caravan trip, except the road was bumpier, a lot wider, and the few 'trucks' on the road, were sometimes as big as floating skyscrapers. We also had the added fun of watching bits fall off the yacht and crucial equipment decide to stop working at odd times. The yacht was built in 1971, and had been all over the Pacific with its previous owners, but had hardly moved from the Napier marina for over ten years. We owned it for four of those years, but because we live 1600 miles away in Brisbane, Australia, we had only visited to do repairs and take short trips into the bay.

When we set off, it seemed that everything that could go wrong, did go wrong. It was challenging, especially for Phil. I have always loved the ocean and the beach, but this was my first sailing trip. Phil had to do all the important jobs while I spent most of our sailing time trying not to fall off my seat or attempting to make it across the room and into the main cabin without falling down.

One day I will be a seasoned sailor who can tell a sheet from a line. I won't have to keep mumbling to myself 'port is left, starboard is right' or keep asking 'what does that green neon line mean on the radar?' One day I will be a contributing member of our tiny sailing team. Until then, Phil is my hero. He singlehandedly kept us safe and brought me home a stronger and happier person.

We saw dolphins. We found new and exciting towns to visit. We lost track of time. We lost the need to hurry everywhere. We even lost a few pounds.

I hope you enjoy reading about this adventure as much as I enjoyed living it and then living it again by writing about it. Maybe it will inspire you to have your own adventures.

I hope so. Best wishes, Nikki

*Sailing - The fine art of slowly going nowhere at great expense while feeling sick and getting wet*

# Map of New Zealand's North Island

# Of Chaos and Disorder

As we walk along the marina through a forest of yacht masts, shoals of tiny fish skitter in the corners of the water. It is late at night and the reflections on their scales look like flashes of underwater fireworks. A lone seagull walks purposefully across the path, petulant at our intrusion on his recently deserted feeding grounds.

Our yacht is almost last on the left, its wooden bowsprit hanging over the path like an eager pet, and Phil pats it as he walks by, murmuring a quiet greeting. It is the middle of the night and there might be people sleeping in nearby boats. We don't want to wake anyone.

Quietly, we climb on board and start to unlock the boat. Our boat has a centre cockpit which houses all the steering and navigational equipment, including an ancient compass and a 1980's radar system. We climb into this first and find that someone has been here before us. The wooden door slats to the cabin's doors are already pulled out and lying across the seats. I look at Phil in surprise.

He opens the small saloon type door on the right, and we look into the back cabin. It looks like an explosion in a wrecker's yard. Bits of pipe and greasy chunks of metal cover the bedroom floor. Oily tools are spread across the narrow shelf under the windows, and the bed has our stored bags on it. The room looks as if every loose bit of metal has been thrown from the engine room by someone looking for treasure and not finding it.

Phil and I look at each other and I start complaining. 'What the heck? Why did he leave such a mess? And you paid him fifty dollars?' I look at my husband accusingly even though I know he is not to blame.

Phil responds by asking me to lower my voice. Our boat is tied up amongst other boats in a marina and there may be someone nearby who knows the perpetrator, maybe even the person responsible for this mess, and apparently, we don't want to offend them.

I continue to grumble as I bring our bags on board and add to the clutter.

This is what happens when you leave your yacht for a year and have to rely on someone else to help out. This is why we want to take the yacht home to Australia, where we can make our own chaos.

Four weeks ago, we tried to register the yacht, but we needed a number from the engine. We were sixteen hundred miles away in Brisbane, Australia, but the Marine Authority was not at all sympathetic about our 'tyranny of distance' excuse. They wanted every 't' crossed and every 'i' dotted. Without the number, nothing could be submitted.

Phil phoned the yacht club in New Zealand and asked if someone could visit our boat and get the number for us. He offered to pay fifty dollars. All they had to do was to walk over to our boat, unlock the door, open the engine compartment, find the specified number, and email it to us.

Two weeks and many follow up reminders later, they sent us a number and it was the wrong one.

In frustration, Phil asked for help from a local businessman we knew (i.e. we'd bought a few things from him on a previous visit and he seemed nice). He drove over, collected the keys, boarded the yacht, and supplied the correct number to us within hours.

The first man has obviously done as little as possible and left an awful mess. This is not a great start to our adventure.

I am already nervous about the idea of sailing our yacht from New Zealand to Australia. I am not impressed to arrive and find it ransacked. We are both tired, especially Phil who has driven most of the four hours from Wellington.

It is a whisper past midnight but we have no choice but to clear up all the tools and metal parts so we can make the bed and go to sleep. At least Phil does. The bedroom is a small, deep room at the back, with a low roof. It is mostly taken up with a wedge-shaped bed and there is no room for two people to clean up without bumping into each other. I leave him to it and go left and down into the main cabin, where I sit muttering in the galley and making a desultory effort to clear the living area, which is also messier than we left it.

Phil bought the yacht two years before we were married and has been planning to sail the yacht from New Zealand to Australia ever since. Now we are a couple, I am part of this adventurous plan, but each time I think of the trip, I see us sliding down the side of fifty-foot waves while I alternately beg Phil for reassurance and pray that death will be quick and painless.

Phil reassures me that no waves will be higher than a multi-story building and we can only die once.

Phil bought a ketch because he assumed he would be living the single bachelor life for a while. He says its two huge masts are easier to handle than one even larger one, and he will be able to manage it alone. I hope he is right because I have no idea what to do to help. I have never sailed except on an introductory trip inside the protected waters of Moreton Bay, the idyllic smooth ocean near where we live.

That was a training trip and the yacht was sleek and modern. I spent ten minutes holding the wheel, five minutes helping winch some ropes, and the rest of the time, sipping cool drinks, eating lunch, and enjoying quiet time on the water.

That first yacht trip lasted just a few hours and we had to return to the dock early because there was a raincloud on the way. It is not much experience for someone expected to co-pilot a yacht across the open sea from one country to another.

Phil says it will probably take about fourteen days to cross the 'big ditch' between the countries, otherwise known as the Tasman Sea. I can't imagine being over a week from land in any direction. What if a storm blows us off course? What if it rains for the whole two weeks or the Kraken turns out to be real? We could be tangled in its tentacles and eaten whole. What if we get lost or marooned?

Secretly, I hope we can't make the crossing on this trip. We can only head out into open sea if the weather forecast is good. There is a good chance that the weather between New Zealand and Australia will not suit and we will just have to spend our time here cruising New Zealand's beautiful North-East. I did tell Phil I would rather stay in New Zealand, but he looked so deflated about the idea that I haven't spoken of it since. I wonder how this trip will end as I climb down the ladder into bed.

At one time, this was a fishing yacht and our bedroom used to be a fish hold. Phil intends to make access easier when he restores the yacht to some semblance of its former glory, but for now, we get into our bedroom by climbing down a short awkward ladder. Each time I do, I wonder how long my fifty-five-year-old body will be able to manage this contortion, and what is going to happen when we are out in a rough sea?

I wonder if we are crazy or maybe naive. We are preparing to sail an old fishing yacht through wild waters, and unknown challenges, to fulfil my husband's dream. And right there I have the answer. I wouldn't want to be anywhere else. If he is going, I want to go. If he has adventures, I want to have them with him. If he dies, I want to die alongside him.

Hopefully, it won't come to that.

4

I am so tired I don't mind the thin plastic mattress covered with egg carton shaped foam. I don't even care that the sheets and quilt smell musty because they have been stored in plastic bags for a year. At least they are dry and not covered with oily tools.

Phil falls asleep instantly, but I lie in bed and think about the stories I have heard about previous trans-Tasman crossings.

One family sailed from New Zealand thinking that because Australia was so big, it would be almost impossible to miss. They set off with just a toy compass for navigation. Unfortunately, they didn't miss Middleton Reef. It is an infinitesimal dot on any map and sits bang between the two countries. The family were stranded there for six weeks.

We have taken steps to avoid such risks. We have a navigation program on our computer that zooms in to the tiniest island or protruding rock. In addition, we have a GPS program on both our phones that neither of us can read without glasses, but which makes a good backup. We have a large old built-in compass and if all else fails, we have a satellite phone and can presumably call for help.

What we don't have, is control over the weather. This is a volatile stretch of ocean and prone to storms. Only twenty months ago, seven people on a seventy-foot racing yacht went missing during a storm and never turned up. Maybe they were taken by a Kraken. I hope it doesn't want our boat.

Our vessel is an almost fifty-year-old sailing yacht built low in the water and taller at each end as if it is a giant floating white and rusty banana. Every outside surface is peeling or rust-stained and the portholes are opaque with paint that has been brushed across the edges, then has run in great drips down the plastic glass. This boat would likely scratch the gullet of anything that ate it.

I listen to the small splashes of tiny rivulets of water at the edge of the hull and small clicks from ropes hitting the mast. I have only taken two short trips out into the bay on this boat, but

I have slept here many times. The small noises and gentle movements are peaceful and relaxing and eventually I sleep.

# Up in the Air in a Boat

Two nights later, it is 2.30 in the morning and I am uneasy because my bed is not moving.

For the last two nights our yacht has been moored next to a floating wharf in the marina and rocking gently as a boat should. Tonight, it is on land and balanced on its keel, which can't be more than six inches wide, and it is only stopped from falling by four metal rods, two on each side.

Before we leave, we need to antifoul the bottom of the boat. This involves sanding and painting the hull with special paint that discourages barnacles from hitching a ride around New Zealand with us. Our only option was to have the local crane operator haul the boat out and put it on a stand in their yard for a few days.

It is unnatural for a boat to be on land instead of swaying gently with the currents and tide and the wake of passing boats. It is also unnatural for me to be sleeping thirty feet above a concrete pad and held up only by a few metal rods and the grace of God.

Every time I walk across the cabin, I feel as if I am going to unbalance it and send it tumbling onto the boat next door, setting off a chain reaction like toppling dominos. I sleep uneasily and prepare myself for the inevitable crisis. I calculate the damage if it falls. (When it falls?)

The boat will roll over with a crash and then it will be stopped by the mast hitting the tarmac. My husband is sleeping against the wall where the ceiling sits under the deck and comes down to a few inches above his face. He is already wedged in a three-sided box. A fall will trap him under me and then everything else in the room will be thrown on top of us.

We will be hurt, but probably not killed, and that is what makes it possible for me to sleep at all. It probably won't be fatal. We will just suffer painful injuries that require months, if not years, of rehabilitation.

***

The next day, the boat is still standing, so we finish painting the underside and then I take photos while Phil puts on stickers we have had printed in town. It is a momentous moment. Our yacht is getting a new name. From now on she will be known as 'Manuka' and because she is now registered in Australia, she has Brisbane written in big letters underneath. It seems ironic since she has not been out of sight of Napier since we have owned her.

Then, I notice that the boat is not sitting evenly. One side is off the ground a little.

'Our boat is not balanced on a six-inch keel,' I tell Phil 'it is balanced on the knife-thin edge of a six-inch keel.'

Apparently, it is still no problem for him. He laughs and parrots my New Zealand accent. 'It is more than 'sux' inches and it is perfectly fine.'

'It is 'seex' then,' I say. But he is still not concerned.

I grab a can, the only round thing I can find and show him how the lean makes it roll easily in one direction. 'See,' I say. 'The boat is lopsided.'

'Yes, it is,' he agrees. 'But it's fine. Safe as houses,' he says.

Thanks to Facebook, I have seen houses slide down hills and topple into the ocean. I am not reassured, especially when he disconnects two of the support poles to paint under them. I try to relax. Only two years ago, I painted the bottom of this yacht almost by myself under the same poles, and I came to no harm.

***

The next day, when the boat is lifted back into the water, I should be able to sleep easy, except ... there is still the anxious anticipation of a dangerous trip.

Before we can leave New Zealand, we have to travel up the East Coast of the North Island and around several notorious capes. It is a wild region with some unpredictable currents and tides. I alternate between being excited and petrified.

Phil says that that New Zealand is known for producing good sailors, presumably because if you can handle conditions here, then anything else is a breeze. Literally.

I would prefer my first yacht experience to be on a calm lake somewhere, preferably with a buffet and room service.

I spend our last night feeling nostalgic.

We have been visiting Napier for four years and we have a great view of the marina from our yacht. I will miss the way the light shines over the water and the amber street lights stretch into pendulums of orange starbursts across the bay. From our back deck I can hear music from the clubs along the wharf, and the sound of happy patrons.

I will miss the jumping fish, shining silver, flipping onto their sides to bellyflop loudly in the dusk. I will miss the clouds of tiny fish that skitter the water into fizz as I pass them gathered in the water between the boats. I will miss the friendly seagull that walks briskly along the marina as if it has somewhere else to go.

I will even miss the man with the grumpy dog that lays on the back deck looking like a shaggy teddy bear and growling like a wild dingo.

I will miss the way the summer heat is tempered by cool breezes and the summer sky is a softer blue, and paler around the edges than Brisbane.

I will also miss the Art Deco.

In 1931 there was a serious earthquake in Napier that killed hundreds of people and flattened many of the buildings. As a result, most of the buildings were rebuilt in the same few years.

It is now known as the Art Deco capital of New Zealand and this Weekend is the annual Art Deco festival. Ladies walk around town with feathers in their hair or rounded sunhats, and men wear braces and blazers, with shiny spats on their feet.

Stunning old cars drive by with silver running boards and white wall tyres. A shiny green and wood steam-truck putters through town, belching dark grey smoke.

At the back of a drawer on our boat, we have a striped shirt, a pair of red braces, black and white men's shoes, and a floppy brown ladies' hat, that are remnants of the year we danced in the park during previous Art Deco celebrations. This year the main event takes place a few days after we leave. Bad timing on our part.

I would like to stay, but we haven't a lot of time. In only a few weeks, Phil is due back at work.

He has a fly in/fly out job at a mine in Western Australia and works for a week and is home for a week. He has combined holidays with regular days off and we have six weeks, four of which we will spend sailing. I hope it is enough.

We have had many happy holidays here in Napier, but there is another reason we feel connected to this place. We were married in the yacht club, between the boat pictures and the canoe hanging from the roof. Phil also proposed here.

Three years ago, I was under our boat, painting the hull with bright blue antifoul, when he surprised me with the invitation to marry him. I had paint all over my clothes and in my hair and on my skin. It was very unusual, and very romantic, in a messy, casual sort of way, but not unexpected. We had been seeing each other for a few years by then and I am not sure if I said 'yes' or 'it's about time you asked.'

Since the wedding, we have been here about four or five times, but we have never sailed farther than the bay. Twice we broke down before we left the harbor entrance. One time we made it into the bay but didn't read our charts right. We sailed perilously close to a large partly submerged reef.

Now we are going to sail up the coast and give this yacht a real work out. Phil says it will take three days just to reach our next destination. I am still nervous.

We head to the yacht club restaurant for one last meal. Phil still has a little more work to do on the engine, so I go ahead and order the meal for us both and then wait. And wait. And try not to get too annoyed at Phil for taking so long. It must be important.

The meals arrive and I sneak a few chips and then catch up with Facebook on my phone to pass the time. I am quite proud of myself for being so patient.

When Phil finally arrives, I am tempted to say something witty about how long he has taken but there is something about his expression.

'I was locked in the marina,' he says. 'Why didn't you come and get me?'

It is all my fault. The marina is locked for security reasons and you can't get in or out without an electronic key. I have the key and he has been waiting at the marina gate for the last fifteen minutes. He has been watching me through the window, staring at my unresponsive back, willing me to turn around all that time.

'I am so sorry,' I say. And just like that, he forgives me and we enjoy our meal. This is why I will follow Phil almost anywhere, even to the middle of the ocean between our two countries. Even, if need be, into danger and uncertainty.

# The Longest Day

We are leaving this morning but there is still plenty to do. Phil has been endlessly busy in the engine area. Over the last few days, he has fixed the electrics, the wind and solar generator systems, the water pump, the bilge pump and installed a new toilet.

Every time I get the place tidy, he needs to open more cupboards to get tools, or rags, or cleaning stuff. It gets tiring living in a mess. I know it has to be done, but I have had enough of grease and muck.

At last, he emerges and says it is time to go. He puts his tools in the corner of the main cabin where he can reach them if he needs them and I can trip over them if I am not looking. He says he might need them and who am I to argue with that? This boat is of an age where ongoing maintenance is inevitable.

Phil then suggests we get a new GRIB file from the Internet. This is a file that will tell us about the wind speed and direction for the next few days, and that could be important. I thought we were ready to go, so I sigh and head over to the club with its free internet connection and do my best. I too would like to know whether the wind will be gentle or cyclonic, but nothing goes well. It is beyond me why I am not getting any new files when I try to save them. We have yesterday's six-day forecast, and we glean what we can from online weather reports and we decide that will be enough.

We head over to the neighbouring boat to say goodbye to Rex who is our neighbour in the marina. He has been very helpful with advice and assisted with the few jobs Phil could not do alone, like install the heavy front sail. Phil wants to ask him to come and help with the first part of the trip. He asks what I think.

I do not want anyone to share the small space we have on the yacht, but it would be churlish to say so. I know nothing about sailing, and Phil will have to do everything without help if Rex does not come.

Then Rex decides not to come. He says he is not going to head north yet because the wind is not good, but he tells Phil that we will be alright.

Nine thirty and we are officially away. We call the coastguard and tell him this is a test voyage and we might be back in half an hour. Better to tell him that, than to be embarrassed later if we have to return to the marina. After our previous experiences, turning back is a very real possibility.

We spend the first two and a half hours of our trip motoring. Apart from the constant noise of the engine, it is relaxing and I start to think we can do this. Phil puts up some sail and finally we get some relief from that throbbing tractor engine. This is fun, and I feel pretty good.

Three hours in, it gets even better. There is a silver flash in the water and we are joined by dolphins. Most of them swim in the slipstream at the front of the boat. One little one weaves in and out and across the others, a child playing among the adults and obviously finding the speed of our boat, way too slow. We stand on the front deck marvelling at their grace and agility, and occasionally saying vacuous things like 'Hello little dolphin,' or 'Thanks for joining us.'

These dolphins are white underneath and now and again they turn sideways. Phil says it is so they can get a better look at us.

After twenty minutes or so, something catches their attention and they peel off, one by two, and start bobbing in the sea behind us. I assume they have found some fish. 'Goodbye,' we both chime in unison.

Six hours in, we have almost left the bay. I am starting to feel like a snack but my tummy is also starting to feel upset. I decide to make crackers with peanut butter because I heard that crackers are good for pregnancy sickness. I am not pregnant, but it is all I know about food for nervous tummies. Then I poach a couple of eggs to eat with the last of our salad. I make Phil a cup of hot chocolate and a lemon and ginger tea for me. Ginger is good for upset tummies, isn't it?

Even though I am feeling sicker than a frog in a spin dryer, I feel like eating. I always feel like eating.

We top the afternoon off with a couple of the dark chocolates I got on special just before Valentine's Day.

Two minutes later I am sick overboard, and can't eat anything for the next twenty-four hours.

It is not just the motion of the boat, but the erratic nature of the motion. Side to side, up and down and never in a pattern. One minute we are leaning forward and to the right, and the next backwards to the left. Then we are sideways, backways, and every way except upside down.

Over the next three hours, I am sick a number of times until there is nothing in my stomach but dry retching. I find the only comfortable position is flat on my back in bed with my legs and arms spread out wide to stop me rolling onto the floor or into the wall.

All night I keep returning to this position because it stops me feeling so nauseous ... until it doesn't. Then I have to wriggle around until I find a better position. It is a long night and even longer for Phil who has to do everything himself. Steer, navigate, and go outside to set the sails.

Even the next day I can't bear to be in the cabin too long so Phil has to write the log entries, read the charts, and call the coastguard, as well as all the dirty or heavy stuff like setting the sails and checking the engine has not blown up.

Sometime during the night, Phil wakes me up because the wind has changed and he has to go outside to lower the sails. I have to be awake so I will know if he falls off the boat. I am half asleep but I am petrified. Phil has taught me what to do if he falls overboard. Turn off the autopilot, slow the boat, steer the boat around, and go back for him. I wonder who will be outside looking for him in the dark while I do this.

Even though he has a life jacket and is tied on with a harness, I am terrified that he won't come back. But after an anxious wait, he does return and I, like the supportive wife I am, go straight back to bed, to spend the rest of the night semi-comatose in my bunk, still trying to find my non-sick lying down position.

Apparently, Phil can't find a good position either. When I wake up the next morning, I find that we have hardly made any progress all night. We have been rounding the cape at the outside of Napier's Harbor and because the tides and currents are erratic here, the GPS has been playing up. With no sight of land in the dark, he admits to going in circles all night. He is not impressed when I ask him why he didn't park up.

At 6.30am, I get out of bed and sit miserably in the cabin. I can't eat. I can't read. I can't write. I can't believe I came on this stupid trip.

Phil tries to get some rest while I watch out for ships. Within twenty minutes, the sails start to flap all over the place and I have to call him back up. Even though he must be exhausted, it is probably the longest rest he gets all day.

After he has changed the sails to suit the new wind direction, and turned on the motor to make up for the low wind pressure, he goes back to bed, only to emerge within five minutes. He has a feeling he should check the engine temperature. The engine is fine but he finds it hard to relax and doesn't go back to bed all day.

16

After a few more tries at getting the sails at a good angle, he takes them down and we just motor. During the morning, he tries a few more times to get some rest but there is always something that needs doing and I don't know how to do anything, even if I was feeling less bilious.

I have been no use on this trip so far and yet I am worn out. My biggest challenge is getting to the bathroom when just being in the cabin makes me feel ill. Every time I get all the way to the front to use the facilities, I come back and am sick overboard. Phil suggests that now he has seen the worst of me, we have no illusions. I suggest he keep his thoughts to himself.

After a morning of sitting by the window, trying to guess which way the waves will toss the boat and failing miserably, I give up trying to be brave and go back to bed. I take a bucket with me and don't spend much time out of the cabin all day.

As well as having my arms out to stop me rolling about, I have all the pillows we have, wedged in various positions around me like doorstops. I spend half the afternoon moving them around just so I can roll over. The rest of the time, I am checking the bucket is still there.

In the late afternoon, I move the bucket aside and sit up. I don't feel any better but I can't sleep any more. Suddenly the boat throws me forward and I hit my head on the bedroom cupboards. Because the room is narrow, the next wave sends me rebounding and I hit my head on the back wall.

'Are you okay?' Phil says.

'I bumped my head,' I say. 'Both sides.'

'Lucky it is nothing important,' he says.

I lie back down. I haven't the energy to fight back.

It is a long, boring, uncomfortable day for me, but at least I sleep through most of it. Phil must be weary to the bone, but he keeps on checking the course, setting the sails, and making sure I am okay.

He is worried that this might put me off sailing forever. I can see how he might think that, but I am not giving up just yet.

As bad as it is, it still beats watching someone else do this on TV. We are having adventures. We are stretching ourselves, physically, mentally, and emotionally. We are pushing our limits and we are obviously crazy, but I am very happy being crazy.

We are out here and doing something. Many people live their lives to be safe. Too many of us watch life through our television sets or computer screens instead of getting out and being part of it.

I am just congratulating myself on making the most of life, when I have to get up again to be sick in the bucket.

I lie down again and spend ages trying to come up with a description for the motion of the boat and decide on this. It is like being on a roundabout, on the back of a truck that is driving over a bumpy hill on a windy road. Only less comfortable.

# Keeping Busy at Sea

I must have slept through most of the night because it is 7am before I am fully conscious. The sea is still so choppy, that even the horizon is a jagged line. The swell is four to five feet high. It doesn't seem that much but it is the action of wind, waves, and swell that is still so unpleasant.

Despite the agitation of the ocean, there is a little wind, so Phil puts up the sails again and then has a well-earned rest.

I sit and stare at the waves coming in and wonder what I am going to do for four hours. He has been awake most of the last twenty-four hours so he needs a reasonable sleep. I feel a little less as if my insides are trying to jump out of my body and now it is just a few dry worms, swishing around in my rubbery stomach. It is an odd feeling since I haven't eaten for over a day.

The waves look much more substantial, and stickier than water usually looks. Thick and gleaming in the sunlight, and tossing the sixteen-ton boat around as if it is a heavy rubber duck. We are not quite cresting the waves because the weight of the boat pushes it through the peaks, but the motion is still jumpy.

Water splashes against the side of the boat, and splatters into white foam. I hang out the side to get as much air as possible and occasionally get wet foamy spray over my shoulders. I don't mind being slightly wet. It is late summer here and still warm during the day. I realise with surprise that I also don't feel nervous. Just seasick again … and bored.

Before we came, I thought I would spend my free time with a novel or reading travel books on my kindle. I imagined myself lounging on the front deck with cold drinks and warm snacks. Today, anything that requires focus brings bile up in my stomach. Even a trip to the bathroom still makes me ill. I mourn the loss of some of my favourite pastimes, reading, writing, and, of course, eating.

I have nothing better to do, so I spend half an hour working out the best way to hold on so I don't get thrown around. I settle on one hand gripping a pole, and the other wedged under my arm and clutching the side tightly. One foot is on the ground and one braced on the seat.

I spend time considering how lucky I am to have Phil. I have a whole new appreciation for my action-man husband as I have watched him hang from the foredeck, setting up sails with both hands while he clings to the deck with his feet, knees glued to the mast. Especially when it is also dark and hard to see, and the waves are trying to throw him in all directions.

As the time passes as slow as molasses, the waves and swell begin to build up until I am sure that some of them are now six feet tall. Land seems so far away and we are heading for the notorious East Cape. What happens then? I already feel the waves trying to tip us over.

To distract myself, I watch cloud shapes along the horizon. I might be a little delirious because I can definitely see an 'S' and if I try hard, I can turn it into 'SOS'.

A few minutes later I read 'Joe' and then 'Please' but that is a bit of a stretch. Because I have 'old people' eyes, I am used to reading blurry writing, but even I have to admit this is a bit unlikely. Soon, even that form of distraction is gone as the clouds along the horizon blur together and form a long line of indistinct haze.

I listen to someone else's report to Marine radio, and they sound so correct. 'Niner, niner, fiver, this is Desolina, Desolina, Desolina. I repeat Desolina.' I imagine an older man with a very correct and borderline compulsive personality.

I look for the expensive bottle of anti-nausea drops I bought before the trip and find it rolling around on the floor. I dab some behind my ears. It didn't work when I used it earlier, so I also put it on my temple, and forehead. It still doesn't work.

I indulge in more wave watching as I try to predict which one will be the next to spray into the rear cabin.

I wonder why visibility is so poor on boats. The windows at the front are not big, and in front of them are masts, ropes, two ladders, and of course sails. How is anyone supposed to see? Every now and then I stand up to look around and make sure we are not heading for any other boats. I have to stand on tiptoe in three different parts of the cockpit to see all around.

This is the way my whole morning goes, making up stuff to pass the time and bobbing up and down squinting at the horizon. I wonder why I ever said 'yes' to this and how we ever expect to get to Australia when I am so sick, tired, uncomfortable and bored.

In the afternoon, Phil is in charge again so I have another sleep. I don't know for how long. Time begins to seem meaningless. Who cares if it is 2.30 or 4.30 when it will still be three more days before we can stop and the floor stops bouncing around? The only time I am not feeling sick and sore is when I am asleep.

All afternoon, I wake up again and again. I can't get comfortable so I give up, get out of bed and wedge myself back into my corner. I have never been elegant or ladylike, but this is ridiculous. My legs are braced at an ungainly angle, my hair is constantly tangled by the wind, and any lingering apple shampoo scent is overlaid with salt.

I am wearing track pants for comfort and warmth, an old but warm woolly jumper, and my oldest shoes. Luckily Phil loves me for me. I wouldn't impress anyone just now. When it gets rainy or cold, I put on Phil's fluorescent orange work jacket with its reflective silver lining. It just gets better.

I thought sailing was all boat shoes, striped tops, and spotless white pants. Where do those people in magazines sail? Not here and not in a boat like this.

Later in the trip, when these experiences are softened by time, I will remember this day fondly as part of my initiation into the life of a real sailor. When I am sipping cool drinks in a beautiful bay, I will not regret one moment of discomfort that it took to get there. In fact, as in most cases, trials like this make the experience more meaningful.

I do another stretch of boring watch while Phil sleeps and then when he gets up, he has good news. He suggests we stop in Gisborne, only hours away. I am thrilled. I could not imagine how Phil would get through another night sailing alone. I am more like cargo than crew. I can't even fill in the log book, or steer the boat without the sails flapping and carrying on like banshees.

It will be dark when we arrive, but Phil has been into port in the dark before. He is confident, but I remember a story he told me about one of his previous trips into port in the dark. He says that a voice came over the radio asking a small boat to get out of the channel as there was a freighter coming. He could see nothing but blackness and decided it wasn't him. Then the voice became more urgent and so he looked up to see lights way up above him. The blackness ahead of him, was the front of a huge great ship and he was the small boat blocking the channel.

I don't want that to happen to us so I decide it might be best if I put my contact lenses in so I can be a second pair of eyes for our late-night entrance into Gisborne.

Putting a tiny piece of plastic into my eye while riding on what amounts to the equivalent of a fairground ride, has seemed beyond my skills until now. Everything has been slightly blurry all day and that suits me because all there is to see is the sea anyway. That might account for why I have a slight headache. Unless that comes from banging my head on the cabin walls. Or being tossed around all day.

For the next few hours, I sit watching the headland that is the entrance to Gisborne and it never seems to come any closer. There are now waves on top of swell and some of them look as if mini-Matterhorn's coming at us. Tiny tsunamis, lifting our sixteen-ton boat as if it was a bath toy. Swells and valleys, making our progress to dry land and firm ground, slow.

Suddenly my phone chimes in with a message. We must be close to town if the phone is connecting. I look at the screen and a friend from Napier has sent a message:

> *Good luck with your trip. I hope you get*
> *safely back on Terra Firma. The more Firma,*
> *the less terror.*

I reply in kind. I will be much happier when we get into port.

When we get around the headland, it is still several miles to the port, and it will take us hours, especially in the dark. Phil picks out two big lights in the direction of the town, and I steer for them. As we get closer, they turn into four big lights and I wonder what it is. A bridge maybe?

There is a strange looking building to the left of the lights, with all the windows lit up. A high-rise office is not what I expected from a small town like Gisborne.

An hour later, when we are a little closer, Phil is the first to notice the obvious.

The four bright lights with a well-lit building is not part of the town. I have been steering the boat straight into a huge tanker that is moored in the centre of the bay.

As I turn the boat to go behind the tanker, I can only wonder what the crew on watch were thinking about us heading straight for them. Phil laughs.

'They must be shaking in their boots,' he says. 'Even sixteen tons of us would feel like a gnat to a tanker like that.'

We keep following the channel marked on our GPS and looking for a green starboard light to the right of a red port light. Phil says that when we see the channel it will be lit up like a runway.

I can't see the runway, even when I am in it. The brightest red and green lights are the wrong way around. There are green lights without red, and red without green, and none of them are where I think they should be.

In the dark. I am struggling to see anything.

'There it is,' says Phil.

'Where,' I whine. 'I can see a red light on our left, but where is the green light?'

'We just passed it,' he says and I groan. I didn't even see it. Now I can see the right lights ahead, but my sense of distance is off. In the dark, I can't tell if they are small lights, or big lights in the distance.

With Phil guiding, and me steering and constantly reminding him that I can't see much, we sail quietly ahead until we reach a small channel leading into the area, he has marked out for us to anchor. Next to the commercial wharf is a large open area surrounded by a stone wall. The water here is smooth as it is well protected from the ocean swell and, even better, it is completely empty.

Both of us are so pleased to be stopping. Phil heads out to drop the anchor while I keep an eye on the GPS and try to keep the boat facing in one direction.

The boat swings as Phil tries to lower the anchor, but I keep studying the map.

Phil comes back in to ask me to stop looking at the map and try to keep the boat into the wind. 'But babe,' I say. 'This is a swinging area.'

He takes a closer look at the map. 'It is indeed.'

We are trying to anchor in a space reserved for the big boats to turn around. Both of us can imagine how well that would go over with the big boys. A little yacht right in the middle of their turning area.

Instead of relaxing and going to sleep, I have to stumble through the darkness again while Phil goes out front to pull up the anchor. Then he guides us further up the channel into the marina while I ponder on the possibility of there being a sign on the jetty that says 'Overnight parking' or '8 hours only'. Of course, there is not.

Why can't yacht spaces be more like car spaces?

I steer the boat carefully into the marina to turn around and Phil says 'Watch out for the pole.'

'What pole?'

'The one with the bright orange cone on top.'

I don't see it until we are up really close. I think Phil finally believes me when I say I can't see much in the dark.

There are no obvious parking spots, so Phil takes the wheel and turns the boat back around the pole and heads back out of the channel. I suspect he has enough of me saying, 'I can't see anything. Really, I can't.'

In ten minutes, we make it to a spot just outside the channel, where I still can't tell if we are anchored next to a darkened supertanker, or a blank wall.

There is a little side to side motion out here where there is less protection, but it is not bad. After the last few days of being thrown around, a little rocking is quite relaxing.

Phil drops anchor and we are both asleep within minutes.

# Gisborne. Back on Dry Ground

When I wake up, we are more remote than I expected, given that we were dodging boats in the channel and there were container ships all over the place. We are around the corner from the main docks and separated from container ships by a low wall.

I can see on the map that town is close and I am pleased. We call the marina and book a berth for the night and then sail in. It looks much less scary in the day time. I expect the marina staff to be surprised and impressed that we arrived, given the ocean conditions were so bad. I expect shock and amazement at our bravery, but no one says anything. I think perhaps the ocean we experienced is normal for this area. Perhaps, my inexperience is showing and this is normal for this region.

Although I lived in New Zealand for most of my life, I have never been to Gisborne and am looking forward to seeing the town, but first we have to get the sail repaired. Sometime during the night, it ripped along the reefing line where it gets tied when it is not fully up.

There is an upholstery place in town and they will do it for us, but they are over three miles away and that is too far to walk today, especially carrying a large, heavy, and badly rolled up canvas sail. We order a taxi and I am very happy when the taxi turns out to be a van. Even though it is old and looks as if it has had a close encounter with a sledge hammer, it is convenient. I forgot to tell the taxi company we had a sail with us. This trip might have been awkward in a car.

New Zealand is expensive for taxis, but I am still surprised when the fare is twenty-nine dollars just for three miles. Then we have the lady wait for us and take us back, so we end up paying fifty dollars all up. It is an expensive repair before we even get the sewing bill. I take a chance and ask if the upholsterer can drop the sail back to us afterwards, and the upholsterer says it is no trouble. I wonder if we could have saved ourselves the taxi fare and asked them to pick it up, but it is too late now so I don't ask. Best not to know.

I checked the Internet before we left the yacht and there are only four things in Gisborne that have been flagged as worth a visit. The museum is one, the hill beside our yacht is another and the other two are too far away. We ask the taxi driver to drop us at the museum.

There are two buildings side by side, so we start with the war museum. There are displays for each of the wars that locals have taken part in: World Wars 1 and 2, Malay, Vietnam, and Korean wars. In the centre of the room is a large red spiral shaped display with the pictures of almost all the local war casualties. It is very sad, to stand inside that display and see the faces of so many young people who died in the prime of life. Some look excited, some look naïve, and others look almost angry, as if they were there under protest.

Next door, at the main museum, the first thing we see is not the Māori exhibit or the local history exhibit but, surprisingly, a Bob Marley exhibition, all dreadlocks and bright colours and reggae music. Not what I expected of a provincial New Zealand town.

There are the usual Māori displays, and historical pictures of the area, but the best display is set in the wheelhouse and cabins of an old ship. The whole thing was salvaged by a local, who dragged it to his home using a steamroller to pull it down the main street, and then he set it up as a house for his daughter. She kept it so well that it looks almost as good as new.

The captain's cabin is amazing. I would love to poke around more. There are so many drawers in his room and after a few days at sea, I can see that drawers would be very handy on a ship. He even has a drawer that folds down into a desk.

On our boat, we have lots of oddly shaped cupboards that make use of spare spaces in the hull, but are just dark recesses. We are still looking for a missing deodorant that has probably rolled into a dark corner somewhere. I make a mental note to ask Phil to make lots of drawers when he restores the boat.

The other thing that surprises me about the captain's cabin, is that the bed is so narrow and has no sides. It is a very good-sized room, bigger than most bedrooms, and there is plenty of space, so why the narrow high bed? If this was the bed on our yacht, there would almost certainly be a large body-shaped dent in the floor next to the bed by now.

Our bed is wider and lower, and if we need it there is a net that can drop down from the ceiling to the mattress to stop us from falling out. When I first saw it, I wondered what kind of maniac would go sailing in weather where you needed to be tied into bed. Now I realise we might be that kind of maniac. When we are in the middle of the Tasman Ocean we can't just pull into a layby if the weather turns bad. If we get fifty-foot waves, I might be glad of a net.

Next, I persuade Phil to walk around to a spot underneath the front of the museum so I can get a geocache. Geocaching is a sport I have been doing for a few years now. You use your GPS to find a location where someone has hidden a small container that holds a log that you sign to say you found it.

There are millions hidden all over the world and listed on the official geocache website. This one is a little canister hidden under the museum building. We find it quickly and sign it.

As we walk back, I tick off more things from my 'to do' list; firstly, phone credit. I want to look up some more geocaches and Phil needs to get weather information.

Then we find a bank. Phil has just been paid, so although the yacht has cost us an arm and a leg, and our credit card is running hot from overuse, we are able to withdraw some cash from our Australian account and buy ourselves something to eat.

We choose a milkshake each and some chicken chippies, then sit on a bench feeling like middle-aged teenagers. We are well past the age when we can eat junk food and not see it in our tummies and on the scale within minutes, but it still reminds me of those carefree days of youth when we I ate what I wanted instead of what was 'good for me'.

At a discount store, we buy a five-dollar pair of gloves for Phil. The skin on his hands is suffering from the strain of hauling ropes and setting sails. The gloves go on our credit card as it ticks it way up to the five-figure mark.

Before we sailed, we bought some expensive safety equipment for the yacht, like new life jackets and a life raft. We could easily have afforded a few trips on a catered cruise ship with the money we spent, but the original fittings were twenty to forty years old. It was worth the money to update the things that our life will depend on if we have an emergency.

As we walk back to the marina, I make another small detour to get a second geocache. Phil is so tired; he can hardly walk and sits as he waits. I didn't think about all the sleep he missed and now he is bone tired and a little wobbly. I persuade him to take a shortcut back along an unused rail track that curves out over the river. Phil turns back several times to make sure I do not trip on the odd wires that stick up in places. Each time, I worry that he is going to slip himself, he is so tired. There are rusty nails and cross bars between the rails, and we need to be careful. I have a mad desire to go 'Choo Choo' but I don't because we are not the only people walking along the rail track. It is a popular shortcut.

We are both sore and tired. By 6 pm, Phil is asleep. I update my diary, read a book, and I think I stay awake right up to 7.30 pm.

# Up the Hill and Down at the Laundromat

This morning we have a very slow start. We have to wait in Gisborne for the sail to be repaired, so we decide to do some more sightseeing and visit the nearby hill which is Gisborne's second claim to fame.

It is a high hill, and a good steep walk, but worth it for the views. At the top of the first rise, there is a statue of James Cook that is not a statue of James Cook. Apparently, it was given to the town and installed before someone pointed out that he had on the wrong uniform and in any case did not look like other pictures of James Cook. Red faces all around, but the statue has stayed in place with a new plaque explaining the situation.

Nearby is a small tree with another plaque. While baby Prince William was crawling after an iconic New Zealand Buzzy Bee toy, Princess Diana planted a Pohutukawa tree, a tree known as the New Zealand Christmas tree for its bright red flowers that bloom in December.

While I love the statue story and the idea that Princess Diana was here, I love the view more and spend ages taking photos. It overlooks the bay from the open sea to the left, across green/grey hills and to the main town and port on the right. A river snakes through the town and between the same factories and stores as most New Zealand towns. Even from here I can see Bunnings, The Warehouse, and signs for all the usual takeaways and phone companies.

There is even a geocache hidden in a tree here. Score four of four for this spot.

Further up where I stop to catch my breath, there is a playground and gym equipment for the energetic. I do what I always do when confronted with evidence of my lack of fitness, and resolve to eat less and exercise more. Then I wonder how many times I have made this commitment and whether I mean it this time.

Further along again we come across an abandoned gun placement, all cracked concrete and damaged railings.

Past that, there is another geocache. It is up on a steep rise between the road and a huge drop off over the ocean. I read on the website that many people have raved about the location, so I figure I have to see it.

When we get to a spot just below the cache, we have two possible ways to get there. One is next to the top of the steep ocean cliff. I choose the other track. It is also steep, muddy and slippery, but the risk of sliding into a small ravine, seems better than the risk of plunging several hundred feet onto the rocky ocean shore.

I make it half way across the slope before I get stuck. I am frozen, one foot wedged into a slight depression and the other threatening to slide. I am staring at the muddy ravine below, and unable to move forward or back. Phil walked across without any trouble, but then Phil used to be in the army. He used to do this sort of a trek in the dark, with a ten-ton backpack, and after three days in wet clothes, without sleep, and with foot long spiders hanging in his path. At least that is what I think he said.

'You can do it,' he says. 'It's easy. You will be fine.'

After this encouragement, I leap gracefully across the rest of the slippery slope.

At least, that is what I wish I had done. Instead, I drop to all fours and crawl slowly and awkwardly, inch by muddy, slippery inch, across the last few sections of slope.

Phil pretends not to notice the mud on my hands and knees and begins to look for the geocache. I am feeling rather defensive. 'Who put a geocache here? What if people bring their kids here? This is a dangerous place to bring people.'

Phil just keeps looking while I turn over a few branches and make suggestions like 'It won't be there. It is too close to the edge.'

When Phil finds the cache, exactly where I said it wouldn't be, we go back the other way. We are less likely to slip, but more likely to die if we do. I will not give that cache a good review.

Back at the yacht, we take the washing to a laundromat, and then I stay with it while Phil goes to buy diesel for the yacht from a local petrol station. As our washing whirrs away, I make friends with a local man who is quite chatty.

He tells me he does not have a job, and then why he does not have a job, both in great detail. He tells me his opinions on Australian politics, and local politics, and the local industry. He tells me that Gisborne will fall apart if the logging industry goes. It is all they have.

My new friend tells me he worked in the mines for a while and I tell him about Phil and how he is my second husband. He asks if I am happy. Too right I am.

For thirty minutes we trade opinions on the state of the world and he tells me personal details about his life, and then when Phil walks in to see how I am doing, he gathers his washing and walks off without a word.

I wonder if he thinks Phil will be mad with him for talking to me. I mentioned he was Australian. Did that scare him? Perhaps he is just rude and I have found the reason he cannot keep a job. Phil says he thought he had a chance with me. Hah. I told him I was happy with Phil. Plus three days at sea have not improved my middle-aged ordinariness.

Phil has diesel all over his hands and one more twenty-gallon drum to fill, so I manhandle the washing most of the way back to the yacht until Phil has finished carting diesel cans back and forth and comes to help.

On our return to the yacht, Phil disappears into the bilge and starts working on the engine yet again so I decide to walk into town. We only have an hour until the sail guy brings the sail back and he wants to be paid in cash. We didn't get enough money out. I had better go and get some.

I have been craving some fresh green juice. Celery, spinach, and green apple would be nice. Maybe some carrot and ginger. We don't have a refrigerator on board so our cupboards are filled with food that can survive a damp yacht for two weeks without refrigeration. The only fresh thing I have is a slightly spongy apple.

The lady at the fishing club has recommended a juice shop, but I find it just five minutes after it has closed. I feel very hard done by. Most of Gisborne seems to be closed. Like many small towns, most people go home at 5 pm.

Luckily, something called the 'Dream Shop' is open later than most and I get most of the other things I need. Hooks to stop bags slipping, non-slip mats for the seats, even ear plugs. This morning we were woken too early when a fishing boat warmed up its engine for half an hour before he left the marina. Ear plugs would also reduce the annoying engine noise of our not very well named 'sailing' boat.

When I get back with the money and the bag, I have only minutes to spare. The upholsterer is due any minute. I sit myself at the front of the building so that he can't miss me. The he calls and I don't hear my phone. He sends a message to say he is under the bar canopy. That is where I am and there is no one else there. Phil arrives and I walk with him to the other end of the bar where we see our sail leaning against the wall.

I call again and the man appears from inside. After we pay him, we take the sail back to the yacht, where Phil disappears back inside the bilge.

34

In the late afternoon sun, I spend the next half an hour, sewing up the sides of the canvas canopy around our yacht. The zip has been hanging off in places since before we left. I naively thought I could sit around doing it while we sailed. That hasn't been possible, so I set to and carefully sew up a whole side and a half with the very expensive thread I got last time I was doing this job. It is punishing work and digs into the flesh of my fingers, but I am proud of the secure way I have stitched it with extra back stitches.

As night falls, we arrange to meet Dave and Ruth off the boat 'Desolina'. They are a young couple from Yorkshire who left Napier after us and, because they are on a lighter and faster yacht, they arrived in Gisborne before us. Dave is the very correct voice I heard over the radio the other day and assumed was an older man.

Over a few drinks at the club, they show us the program they use to predict the wind patterns and plan their routes. They tell us they bought their yacht a few years ago and lived on it in Wellington before setting off on their trip just a few months ago. That is just a few months more sailing than we have done.

For a young couple, I decide they have a great attitude to making the most of life.

We are all leaving in the morning, so we head back to the boats before it is even dark and Phil and I are both asleep by eight o'clock. It must be the sea air.

During the night I wake up and think I smell smoke. I get up and there doesn't seem to be anything to worry about so I write 'buy smoke alarm' on my list of things to do and go back to bed.

# Gisborne to Tauranga

We are heading out again today, so I am reluctant to wake up and even less enthusiastic about getting out of bed. I briefly consider whether I could catch a plane home. This is my first experience of sailing and it has been miserable and made me sick. Am I crazy?

Phil has been up for over an hour, getting the boat ready, and of course is now back in the bilge, greasing something, or tightening other things. He will need help to get the sail back on, so I have no choice but to get up.

I fix a few screws to the walls, rinse a few towels, and put some more bungee cord on the canvas doors to hold them down in the wind. Then I head for the club to play on my computer. I want to load the program that Dave and Ruth recommended, but nothing goes to plan.

First, the program plays up, then the computer wants to update itself, and then when I get it all sorted, I realise I did not bring my credit card to pay for it anyway.

When I arrived at the club, I was the only patron so I set myself up in a quiet corner next to a power outlet. By the time Phil comes two hours later, there are scores of people here having lunch. Someone has opened a door behind me and diners pass my formerly secluded table in cheerful clumps.

Someone moves a chair from my table to get a wheelchair past. Then a lady with crutches stumbles around the same chair. I try to be gracious and helpful, but each time I move the chair, someone moves it back again.

I have spent nearly two hours at my laptop with nothing to show for it and am not looking forward to setting off on the next leg of our sick-making, people-tossing, yawn-inducing yacht trip. I tell Phil it is not going well and we decide to have lunch at the club.

After prawn cutlets with chips and salad, I am in a better mood, but I wonder if fried food is the best last meal for a woman condemned to the sea's tossing and heaving.

By the time we set off it is almost two o'clock. I have been dragging my heels, and am in no hurry. Our late start will mean we spend more time at sea in the dark but Phil doesn't seem worried about that.

I am feeling a little more confident about setting off now and I am in charge of freeing us from the jetty. The ropes all come loose easily and we are away with no fuss at all.

As we motor down the marina, I wave to a couple of friendly fishermen. A few minutes later, we turn around and go back, passing them again. We have forgotten to leave the key for the marina.

As we approach the dock and I prepare to jump ship with a rope in one hand, and hang up the key with the other hand, the harbour master arrives.

I aim carefully and toss it lightly into his hands. He looks dreadfully nervous when he realises what I am about to do, but he catches the key without losing it in the ocean and we head off again. No sign of the fishermen.

The first part of the trip is not too bumpy and we are running along at five to six knots. I feel well enough to nibble on a couple of ginger biscuits and then make some soup in a cup. With the stove swinging lightly, it is quite a challenge, but after two days on land, I am feeling better, and it is nice to be able to eat at sea again.

As we head away from land, the sea becomes sloppier. Waves and swell, seem to come from all directions. I don't feel too sick, but I do have a headache. I think it is the engine. We do a lot of motoring for a sailing ship.

We head out further away from the shore, so that Phil can have a clear run through the night. Watching land get further away is discouraging but there is a surprising diversion.

There are yellow and black balloons in the ocean.

Phil says that each one is attached to a line and is a crayfish pot marker. He says the line could tangle in our rudder if we don't see it in time. I am steering the yacht, so watching for markers keeps me amused for the next few hours while Phil works on the autopilots.

Neither the manual, nor the automatic autopilots seem to be working properly. It keeps Phil busy for some time. I wonder when the relaxing part of sailing starts. Phil told me sailing would be quiet and peaceful with lots of time to read and sunbathe. Instead, he is always setting the sails, or working on something, and I am bored silly. Watching for crayfish pots is hardly stimulating.

At 7.45 pm I find it hard to settle. Phil has a long night ahead and the boat is making horrible noises. I head for bed, but not to sleep. The wind is gusting, and falling, and throwing the boom around. Things bang against the mast, and the sails and ropes flap and slap against each other.

I wonder if I would get more sleep if a herd of elephants was practicing ju-jitsu next door.

I put in the ear plugs I bought but they don't help much. Phil gets the autopilot to work and climbs into bed with me. Then he gets back out of bed and then in and out of bed like bread in a hotel toaster. The radar alarm goes off to say that there is a boat coming into our twelve nautical mile zone. It goes off to say that there is a boat leaving our zone.

There is a lot of banging from the boom as it tries to swap sides in the wind. The sails flap and carry on as they adjust to the change.

At some point, he gets up and puts away all the sails. I have to be up for this and worry that he might not get back inside safely. Then, since neither of the autopilots seems to be working, Phil turns on the motor and sets himself up to steer all night.

It is hard to sleep with a tractor engine just a few feet from my head and every surface throbbing and vibrating in unison, including my head.

I wake often. Then somewhere in the dead of the night, I am startled awake when I feel the boat turning. I sit up suddenly and hit my head. I have been sleeping on Phil's side of the bed, wedged into the three-sided box that is half our sleeping space. I am convinced the boat is going off course. Where is Phil?

I panic. I have vague memories of Phil saying he was going outside to check something and I was so sleepy, I didn't even get up. Did he make it back?

I get up to check and am excessively relieved when I see Phil, still hunched at the wheel.

Phil has changed course because there is a fishing boat coming up behind us. Even with a small running light at the top of our mast, we are hard to see. Even harder to see, if everyone on their boat is a sleeping fisherman. They are probably running on an autopilot that actually works, so Phil has decided not to risk a collision and is moving well out of their path.

When I wake up for the last time, I find him hunched against the wall in a foetal position, with his feet on the steering wheel and his head against his chest. He has become our autopilot.

'Are you okay?' I ask.

'Yes fine,' he says. 'I got a bit of sleep here and there.'

# Rough weather and I need Crampons

Despite being so positive, Phil has had a bad night, huddled against the wheel, feet keeping the boat on track, and still not getting very far. I don't feel too bad this morning, so I manage a little shower, and have a drink of water before taking over for Phil for a while so he can sleep.

We are still not getting very far, and certainly not fast. We are doing 3.5 knots. Even I can walk that fast.

We are still motoring because there is no wind and I am disappointed. For a short while yesterday, we were doing 6-7 knots, and using our sails.

To pass the time, I spend hours staring out the window. Sea birds visit occasionally to see what we have on offer. Most boats in the area are fishing boats, so they hope for fish scraps, but we don't even have food crumbs.

Skimming across the water, these birds look as if two stalks of dark brown flax have been tied together at a small twig body. When they see nothing of interest on our boat, they set off again on their long hunt.

When Phil wakes up, I make us porridge and yoghurt again. Our yoghurt has soggy labels from sitting in melted ice for a few days, but still seems edible. It doesn't make us sick anyway.

A tanker appears, causing me some anxiety, but it is heading off in another direction.

Phil drops back into the bilge to do yet more engine maintenance. I don't know how we would cope if he wasn't mechanical by trade, and resourceful by nature. The engine needs more attention than a pre-schooler.

Most of the morning, we have to motor; the noisy whine of the engine drumming into our heads. Then the wind picks up and we set the sails. At least Phil does. Balancing on the deck as it bounces up and down.

With the wind and the sails going together, the boat starts to heel over badly. The right deck is nearly in the water, but we are moving along well so we leave it for a while.

It goes like this for hours and both of us start to feel like lunch, but it seems fraught with danger.

Phil would happily fix lunch for us, but he is steering the boat and it is kind of important that we don't crash into nearby rocks.

I sit watching the cabin door for a while, trying to guess which way to lean first. With the swell going one way and the waves another, there is no easy way to work out my next move.

'Right. I am going in,' I finally say.

'See you on the other side,' Phil says in his best impersonation of a space captain sending his first mate in to battle moon monsters.

I lurch through the cabin door and fall down all three steps. My elbow bangs loudly on the frame and I land awkwardly on the floor.

I am hurt, tired, hungry and a little achy.

'No problem. All good,' I say cradling my injured elbow with my other hand.

It seems easier to give in to the bucking movements of the yacht and just fall onto the cushioned seat on one side. I sit for a while, trying to get up some more courage.

'Right then. Here I go.' I say, more to encourage myself than to keep Phil informed.

I decide to try for cheese and crackers, that should be easy enough.

I use the momentum of the boat to cross to the other side where the food cupboards live. I jam my left knee into the side of the bench seat and brace my right leg against the floor. My uninjured elbow is rammed into the back of the low kitchen wall, and with the other hand I attempt to reach the crackers.

The floor is still sloped to one side and each jarring roll of the boat throws me against my knee or threatens to toss me back against the far wall. The staccato sounds of rope on metal, and sails whipping in the wind distract me. It sounds like a bad movie set, and smells worse. The movement has opened the bathroom cupboard and the faint odour of dead possum has crept into the main cabin.

I lean at a 45-degree angle against the couch cushions to anchor myself while I reach the cupboards. On my second forward lurch, I manage to open the cupboard door. On another, my hand closes around the crackers.

I don't need the whole packet, so I wrestle half of them from their wrapper during a backwards lurch and restore the rest to the container when it comes within reach again.

Then the next wave kicks it up a notch and I am thrown backwards. As if in slow motion, my feet slip on the loose carpet and the carpet and I slide into a messy pile on one side of the room, crackers in one hand, and a fistful of carpet in the other.

When we arrived at the yacht, the carpet was filled with years of grease and grime. It was so bad that I couldn't bear to walk on it without shoes of some sort. Then Phil cleaned it with a pressure washer and laid it out in the sun to dry.

It was already made up of odd shapes and cut out flaps that fit around holes for accessing the under-floor tanks. Since being washed, pieces overlap each other, and bulge in odd places. And it's not stable.

For several minutes it is easier to stay on the floor amongst the bunched-up carpet than to stand up.

I collect more crackers off various surfaces and am surprised when I only have to throw away two of them. Now for the cheese. And a plate. And a knife. This is even harder than I thought.

The cheese is in the old fridge under the map table. The fridge doesn't work but it had ice in it when we left. Now it is just a clammy watery soup, with a floating packet of cheese in it.

It is a real credit to my dexterity that I manage to move the maps, open the fridge, and delve into the watery depths to fish out the cheese, all while holding on to the crackers with one hand and holding onto the walls with my hips and my knees.

I get a plate but forgo the knife. I can rip the cheese slices with my teeth if I have to. Only two days at sea, and I am feeling quite feisty, but not up to carrying a sharp knife in this environment.

By the time I get back to the deck with my offering, I expect a standing ovation, but Phil is having his own problems. Steering in rough sea while trying to keep your balance on a moving bouncy floor, is hard work. We would both love a drink, but there is no way I am going back down below without an ice pick and crampons.

The rest of the afternoon passes slowly. I sit wedged in the low corner of the seat, and get splashed by the occasional rogue wave. I move to the high corner. I get a better view from here, but I am constantly bracing myself with all my limbs and if I lose focus for a few minutes, I slide down to the low end anyway. I have seen playground slides less slippery than this.

I am fascinated by the window on the low side. I have that feeling I sometimes get when on a high ledge, as if I am being pulled over. I can easily imagine that window as a trap door and me sliding right through it into the ocean. I hold on tightly.

Waves constantly cover the front deck in foam, and several times, they break over the roof and slide down the front windows.

When I see a fishing boat go by, I am jealous. It is not being tossed around anywhere near as badly as we are. In fact, it seems quite smooth. Phil says it is because they are travelling with the ocean and wind, and we are heading into it and fighting it.

He suggests I wave to the fisherman, but instead I place my hands on the plastic fabric of the side wall, and pretend to shout for help. 'Save me. I am being carried away by a mad man.'

Phil suggests I could send out an SOS message in a bottle. We have so many empty water bottles now that I could pepper the sea with them. We are both mad together. I wonder for the umpteenth time what I have got myself into. The fishermen are out here because they are getting paid. We have spent a fortune to be this uncomfortable.

Because of all the repairs and the safety equipment we have had to buy, we have the biggest credit card debt either of us has ever had. That money could have paid for several cruises. All food supplied, rooms cleaned for us, shows every night, and a huge ship that laughed at rolling seas.

I am slightly sick, hungry again, and I can't find a steady seat, but even with all that, I am glad I am here. Adventure doesn't come without some discomfort and sometimes a high cost. Sometimes it is even downright painful. I have bruises to attest to that.

Surprisingly, I don't feel at all scared. I feel as if I am in a film called 'Danger at Sea' but I trust this boat to keep us upright, mainly because the keel is so heavy, it will always want to be bottom down. My biggest fear, is of boredom. There is not much I can do, except look out the window and brace myself against the seat yet again.

Phil does most of the steering because it is very hard work. The waves jolt the boat around and the course needs be corrected every few seconds. The autopilot is still flaky, so we spend a lot of time checking the line on the electronic navigation chart and trying to get back to it.

I spend some more of my time changing seats. I would prefer to sit on the high side to balance the boat, but even though I am heavy, my weight is not likely to make any difference to the lean of a sixteen-ton boat. Besides, if I don't brace myself properly, then I just slide to the low side anyway.

After a while, I bravely take over the steering so Phil can sleep. We are rounding a headland and as well as rough sea, there are currents, and tides, and wind to shake things up a bit. It is hard work and slow going, but it passes the time. At least for a few minutes, then the sails start flapping again and Phil has to get up to fix them. It is time to change the angle of the sails and I don't have the slightest clue how.

There is a freighter coming towards us, but he is not too close so we continue with our tacking procedure. Phil goes on deck and I take the wheel. As the boat is not moving, except to drift in the wind, I cannot steer. When Phil says to go left, I turn the wheel as far left as it will go and the boat turns lazy circles to the right, getting close to the freighter.

The oncoming ship, swaps sides and crosses to our left, confused at what we are doing and not sure where we are headed. We are not sure either. Luckily, they seem to have control of their boat. We sure don't.

As the freighter passes, a low voice comes over the radio. 'You like to live dangerously.'

Phil is embarrassed and unsure what to say. I suggest he says he has a learner driver steering. He thinks about it. After several minutes he replies. 'We saw you; we were just trying to change course.'

Well, what else can you say? Some guy on a freighter will go home with a good story to tell tonight. 'Such idiots,' he is sure to say. 'Such a big ocean, and there they were turning circles in front of my fifty-ton ship.'

It is times like this I think we might have been better to have our ships name a little less visible.

Phil spends the next fifteen minutes out on the bucking deck, trying to untangle the ropes that got crossed and twisted as we danced around in the wrong direction.

When Phil says I can turn the boat and get going, we start bounding along at 8.4 knots … in the wrong direction. The wind is still not in our favour. We need to be heading into it. Phil sets a better course with a lot less speed, and then goes back to try to get some much-needed sleep.

As the sun gets lower on the horizon, I am feeling pretty good about being useful for a while, but I realise we need to reduce the main sail for the night. I don't want Phil to be out there at midnight, better to get some sail down now. We will go even slower, but it should save Phil a job during the night.

By the time Phil gets his life jacket on and finds the tie down ropes for the sail, I realise I have left it too late. The dusk turns into dark and there is no moon. Phil is out pulling down the sail and I can't see anything.

He comes back inside to complain that the main sail has ripped right across the reefing line where it was repaired. This time it has gone almost full length. Tying it down is going to be even trickier than usual.

I am at the wheel, trying to steer for a star because it is the only thing I can see. I can't read the compass in the dark and the GPS is slow and, in any case, it turns itself off every few minutes because it is low on battery.

Phil goes back outside to secure the sail at the next reefing line.

Suddenly there is a loud bang, and I look outside to find a long grey post that looks like part of the mast, has fallen to the side of the deck. After a few minutes it disappears. It looks to me as if it has fallen into the ocean. What do we do now? We have two masts, and heaps of spare sails, but that looks as if it is an important piece of equipment.

I can't hear anything but the usual sail flapping outside and I begin to get nervous. I can't see Phil. He has gone back outside, so I check the foredeck. Nothing. On the roof? Nothing. Where could he be hiding? He has been sensible enough to attach himself to the boat with a safety harness, but since I can't see him, I panic.

'Phil,' I call out. Nothing. 'Phil,' my voice is rising and I am starting to tear up. No response. After my third call out, I think I hear something. A few moments later, Phil appears. I am full on crying now and he climbs back into the cockpit and is greeted by a big emotional hug.

I pictured him hanging unconscious off the side of the boat and being towed along in the waves.

He tells me we broke a davit post. So that was that bang. Not an important piece of mast after all. It was part of the structure that was supposed to hold a tender up and hang it from the back of the boat. It has not even been able to hold itself up, so he has tied what's left of it to the rail.

Then Phil has to go back out again because a rope is tangled in the wind generator. I hand Phil the torch and try to get myself together as he heads back onto the lurching deck. At least I can see the torch light as he works and I know he is there.

He takes a long time but he can't untangle the rope in the dark. He decides to leave it until morning and hope nothing gets worse in the meantime. Good idea.

With Phil back inside, it is time to set off in the right direction again, but we can't work it out. The GPS says we are heading backward, but there is a lighthouse on our left that suggests we are facing the right way. We do a few about turns in confusion.

48

Suddenly, I realise that the current is dragging us back. That is why the GPS shows us going the wrong way. We are heading one way and moving another. All we can do is set off in the direction we think is correct according to the lighthouse and hope the GPS catches up. I feel quite proud of working out that little problem, but then I have had about twenty hours more sleep than Phil.

We have decided to stop at the next available anchoring spot and rest. We locate a little cove on the map and head for it. I suggest Phil calls Maritime Radio to report our situation. I think it might be important for them to know where we are. We seem to be in some trouble.

Phil calls it in. 'Maritime Radio, Maritime Radio, this is Manuka.'

'Manuka, this is Maritime Radio. What is your speed and position?'

'Maritime Radio, this is Manuka Victor, Juliet, November, 4783. We are at East 152.43.56, South 27.456.56 travelling at three knots. We have changed our plans and are heading for Hicks Bay.'

'Manuka. This is Maritime Radio. We have noted that. I hope all is well? Over'

Phil does not answer that.

Our sail is ripped, our wind generator has a rope knotted around it, and something fell off the mast. We are limping along against the current, and we are both exhausted. I think maybe he should have let them know we are struggling, but I don't say anything. He is in charge and he knows what he is doing. I hope.

For a while I can't sleep. I don't want to leave Phil out here sailing the boat alone yet again. I watch the moon as it scatters light across the water towards us. I take photos and try to capture on video the sensation of scattered sparkles made by moonlight.

I take charge for a few minutes while Phil has a shower, and then when there is not much I can do, I go to bed and leave him to it.

For now, the autopilot is working, so Phil sets the radio to make sure no one is coming and climbs into bed with me for a bit. All night he is up and down, and once he has to change course to avoid a big ship. Neither of us has a restful night.

# East Cape? Who put that here?

When I wake for the last time, it is a cloudy dawn but over the next few hours the day turns clear and sunny. We have gradually and achingly slowly, passed East Cape and the sea has slowed to a light swell.

We decide not to stop at Hicks Bay and call in Maritime radio to let them know. We are going to keep going since things have calmed down. We are off to White Island, New Zealand's off shore active volcano.

We both have showers. It feels nice to be clean again and it is chance to examine all my new bruises. There is a beauty on my left thigh. All yellow and grey with a black edge. It looks like a dirty ink blot, or the worst tattoo ever.

We are reassuringly close to land, and I am happy we are not running out to sea again. We took a wide swing away from East Cape thinking it would be easier, and I don't think it worked. We seem to have gone the long way around.

In the daylight, and without a torch in one hand, Phil manages to untangle the wind generator and even better, it is not damaged at all. I take photos of the sun coming up and start to enjoy the beauty around me. A seabird lands in the ocean next to us and bobs for fish. The clouds on the horizon look like cotton wool and the sea has a gentle roll that is peaceful, especially after last night.

Mid-morning it gets even better when I spend twenty minutes on deck watching dolphins swim under our bow. There are eight or nine of them, all steel grey and glistening wet as they arch out of the water and back under again.

They are the same grey and white dolphins we saw before, but this time some of them are swimming in pairs, the bottom one upside down and mirroring the top one. Since the bottom ones are marginally smaller than the top ones, I wonder if they are mothers and children.

It is a wondrous thing to watch and lifts my spirits. This is the sort of day that makes even last night seem worthwhile.

I make pancakes for breakfast, grateful I can eat again, and then I have a little sleep. I worry about how tired I am when Phil is the one missing the most sleep. I wonder if my thyroid medication is doing its job. It is supposed to be kept in a fridge but we don't have one.

I wake up dozy and sick of the noise of the engine again. I am pleased when Phil puts up the sails and we can turn it off. We can't head straight for White Island because, as usual, the wind is coming from that direction, but we can tack away for a bit and then turn back. At least this time we don't have to go way out to sea to get anywhere.

I make soup for lunch and it is calm enough that we eat it on our back deck, seated on the bench seat and squeezed in between the ropes and wires.

Later, Phil has a sleep while I read a book.

I am thrilled to be able to read. It is a big accomplishment. A few days ago, I could barely look at a page without being sick over the side. Now I spend all afternoon reading a murder mystery and it passes the time beautifully.

Dinner is another highlight. Fried potatoes and eggs. Some days, meals are all there is to look forward to, and I don't take eating for granted any more.

As it gets dark. I think I can see the island on the horizon, but we have to head away from it to get wind. No surprises there. There is also a star that I can steer for. This is important because the computer has stopped charging.

We are using the ship's ancient inverter to charge the computer with the ship's 12-volt system, but something is wrong. Phil works out that if you jiggle the wires at just the right angle then it will turn on for a bit, but nothing must move around it or it will stop charging again. It is very difficult to keep things still when the ship moves up and down constantly.

We did have a backup plan. Before we came, we bought a 12-volt charger for our modern streamlined computer online, but they sent the wrong part. If we can't charge the computer, we could be stuck with using our tiny phone screens to navigate. It's good to know we have a backup but neither of us has good vision for tiny print. We pray that the computer lasts.

I spend the last part of my evening watching the star that is to help us navigate, dip slowly down until it is lost behind the horizon. At least we have the autopilot. For now ...

# White Island – An Active Volcano

It is another typical night sailing. The sails flap and bang and Phil is up and down resetting the sails or changing our bearing to suit the wind. At one point he gives up, takes the sails down and starts the motor again.

At 6am, I wake up in the little three-sided coffin that is usually Phil's side of the bed. It is claustrophobic. I feel as if I do not have enough air, and the throbbing of the engine is making me edgy. When I can't take it anymore, I have to wake Phil yet again, so we can swap sides. I am still uncomfortable but at least the other side has a slight breeze.

I am not sick, but not well either. I am hot and clammy, and trying to imagine I am on a serene beach instead of inside a fish hold and three feet from a tractor engine. No way can I get the engine out of my head. It vibrates with every part of my body as well as every surface of the boat.

Phil gets up and turns off the engine.

Blessed silence. But I can't get back to sleep. I get up for some peace and walk into a plague of flies.

At first it is just a few, buzzing lazily in the cockpit. This far out to sea, they must have come with us. I only saw one fly yesterday, and I didn't give it much thought. Now there are at least a dozen out in our main cabin and disgustingly, eight more floating upside-down in the washing up water I left to soak the last few dirty dishes in.

I spray the live ones, tip the dead ones overboard, and notice a few taking a free ride on our front deck. I go after them with a rolled-up towel but they are too quick and I only get a few.

By mid-morning and after spraying and swatting for some time, I leave it for a bit, only to find that a few hours later, there are at least fifty flying around the cabins. More spray.

What is going on?

I go outside and there are another hundred squatting on the rolled up front sail. They are settled on the handrails, and along the ropes. We bang and swat, but they have nowhere to go. It is ocean all around us. They just circle back to the boat.

It might be my imagination, but they seem a little slow. As if the motion of the boat is uncomfortable and they can't work out where they are supposed to be. But that doesn't make them easy to catch. The boat is still going up and down like two elephants on a seesaw. There is an added level of difficulty to swatting flies when just standing up without falling is hard.

Eventually we track the source down. They have been procreating in the rubbish bags. The bags have been hanging around for a few days and there must have been just enough food scraps in there to support a nursery of black invaders.

I ask Phil to pass me something to swat with and he passes me a leather glove. It is too hard to find something better so, even though it is very slow going, it helps pass the time. The boat is rolling around and even sitting targets are moving, but it is very satisfying. 'There goes another one,' I crow at intervals.

Phil is more philosophical, and relaxed, but I feel a sense of accomplishment with each one I manage to destroy. The rubbish is now in the hold at the back, so each fly down means we were closer to having none at all.

The sea is as smooth as I have seen it on this trip. We are still rolling from side to side because we are, of course, still heading against the wind, but I decide I should be able to manage a shower.

A shower on a moving boat needs at least three touch points to keep balance. The shower space is not wide enough to spread my feet, so I have to have two feet on the floor, a knee or an elbow against one wall, and one hand against the opposite wall. That gives me one hand to wash with, but makes lifting my feet to wash them impossible.

Dressing is no better. Even in the larger space of the main cabin, I keep falling against things. At least in there it is more likely to be a soft couch cushion than a metal tap.

Pulling on pants is the hardest since I need to lift my feet off the floor. It is a comedy in awkwardness and results in more bruises, including an especially ugly one on my calf.

The sails are up, but I don't get long to enjoy them because the wind is gusting again. The sails are flapping and banging and carrying on like ghosts in a comedy movie. We can't take any chances with one of them damaged. The engine has to go on again and the main sail is pulled in.

The rip across the main sail is especially annoying. We just paid $75 plus the cost of the world's most expensive taxi ride, to have it repaired and it didn't even last for one whole day. Phil says that the word boat means 'bring on another thousand'. We have surely done that. Again, and again.

I am feeling quite confident at sea now, especially with the wind died down and the sea a little calmer. I make scrambled eggs, with potato chunks, and fried tomato. There is some very soft and sad looking cheese left, so I put it in with the scrambled egg. I feel quite pleased with the repast I have whipped up on a swinging gas hob in the middle of the ocean, and we eat it looking out over the water. The sun is coming up and White Island is gradually taking shape in the distance.

White Island is New Zealand's only active marine volcano and of great interest to the scientific community. There is a plume of white steam rising from the top and a ridge of low ground in the foreground. The shape is the classic upside-down cone.

With the sky so blue, it is picturesque indeed and I take scores of photos. I don't want to miss the perfect shot. I take some with Phil in the photo and some showing the front of the boat. Over the next few hours, I jump up every now and again to take another photo. It gets even prettier as we approach and the steam plume changes slightly. As it takes three hours to get there, that is a lot of photos and a lot of jumping up and down.

The island seems to be made of dry rock, but as we get closer, I can see a patch of grass, and another of dead and twisted leafless trees, but I see nowhere to land. I once came here on a tourist boat with three of my sons and there was a small concrete looking landing block here. The last time I came, the sea was too rough to land and now it seems I have missed my chance again.

In all the excitement of being up close and personal with an active volcano, a wind gust catches us by surprise and tears at our sun hats. Mine is strapped on but Phil loses his to the ocean.

Our hats are both ugly, and wearing them makes us look like chunky roofing nails, but they are practical. Phil's is also faded from being in the chlorine in our swimming pool so I am ready to write it off as a casualty of the trip, but Phil has other plans.

He turns the boat and to my surprise, we find it where we left it. I assumed it would float away and be too hard to spot. I make an ineffectual movement with the boat hook as we pass and miss it. I am ready to suggest Phil tries it next time, but he urges me on and turns for another pass.

This time it is a clean grab and I am immensely proud of catching it on the end of our boat hook. I drag it across the front of the boat and present it to Phil for drying. He puts it on his head and suggests it is now a hat with a special story. I decide to call this the 'Black Hat and White Island Adventure.'

The next few hours are some of the best on the trip. As we sail lazily past White Island and then watch it fade slowly into the distance, Phil and I sit on the front of the yacht and sunbathe. Phil makes cheese and tomato on crackers and even with the soggy cheese it is delicious.

I have a bottle of water in the nearby sail holder and I feel like a movie star, or a rich trophy wife, luxuriating in the sun at the front of my yacht. This is the way sailing should be; sunshine and relaxation as the wind blows us along. The water is mildly rocking us and I am sleepy and relaxed. Or I would be. I am still swatting the odd fly off our boat.

Phil and I joke about what foods we miss. We are well stocked but are almost out of anything fresh. The last of our chilled food has been swimming in the melted icebox for days and has had to be thrown out. All I can think, is that ice in my drinks would be nice, and maybe a pineapple ice block. I miss icy food, but not that much. Phil says chicken chips are what he misses. It is not much and we are aware how lucky we are. We are having an ideal time on a beautiful day.

This lasts for hours, but eventually the lack of real wind means Phil has to start the engine yet again.

I sit for a while with my feet over the edge of the boat. The faster trip has made the boat rock further until I can dangle my legs over the side and every now and then, the water comes up to meet them. It is refreshing on such a hot day and I ponder on how we can change the boat to make this more comfortable.

Right now, I am sitting across a metal upright that cuts into my legs. Other people have swimming platforms and hammocks that can be lowered into the water. We have unsafe side rails and rusty metal protrusions everywhere.

Then Phil brings me a boat cushion and some chocolate, which makes me very lucky indeed. He is a treasure and I wouldn't change this for anything.

We were planning to head to a quiet island, but have decided to stop in Tauranga instead. It is a big enough town that there should be someone to repair our sail and a retailer to sell us a new computer cord.

We expect to arrive at Tauranga quite late, so I take over the wheel again so Phil can get some sleep. The autopilot is doing its job, so I get to read again, just bobbing up and down every five minutes to check there are no boats coming our way.

In the late afternoon, Phil gets up. He puts out the sails and tries the Mizzen mast for the first time. It is right at the back, sort of like a bonus sail. He says it will help balance the boat. It feels to me as if it does, and with the other sails and a better than usual wind, we are soon bounding along at 6 knots or more. We are heeled over and the boat jumps around like a skittish new foal, but it is lovely to know we are getting somewhere in a hurry. Much of our trip so far has been at 3 knots.

As a bonus, we are sailing directly to where we want to go. Most of our trip has been a compromise. We want to go north-east, but we have to zig north, then zag east to catch a better angle of wind. We can sail in almost any direction except directly into the wind and even though the jagged coast means we have to change direction often that is where the wind always seems to come from.

I love watching the land come closer and White Island getting smaller. At our usual pace, it took forever to see any change. At this speed, I can even see the red arrow move on the navigation program. We are really moving now.

I am excited enough to make tomato and pasta for dinner. It is a very simple dish normally but not on a boat. The boat is heeling and rolling so much that the boiling water threatens to flood pasta all over the floor. I stand with one leg well back, ready for a quick getaway and try not to fall onto the gas cooker as the whole thing sways wildly. It is supposed to sway to level but it seems much too wild for that.

As we eat the pasta with its can of tomato topping and follow it with small steamed puddings warmed in the hot water, I consider what a long way I have come since we first started out.

On day one, I could hardly even enter the kitchen without being sick, and now I am cooking dinner and enjoying it.

Phil tries to call Maritime Radio to let them know we are stopping at Tauranga, but there is no answer. He calls again twice more as we get closer. It is discouraging when they don't answer. I expect it is our antique equipment playing up again. What if we have a real emergency?

To pass some time after dinner, I make a list of things I would like changed when the boat is restored. Top of the list is bracing for the seats so I don't have to slide down them in heavy weather. I also wish the seats were higher. I love sitting up in the cockpit, but maybe because I am short, I can't see much and have to keep standing up to look for ships. Cushions would be nice too since we use these seats a lot.

Carpet that stays on the floor would be good. A wider bed where neither of us has to sleep under the deck with six inches of clear air space would be nice too. The other day, Phil hit his head three times in a row trying to move around in bed. He keeps saying he doesn't mind but I suspect he is just making the most of things.

I would like somewhere to hang the hammock and most importantly, a real safety line for when Phil has to go outside in bad weather. There is a safety line on the boat now, but it is held together with string and rusty wire. Neither of us trusts it. Phil ties on to the mast or the cockpit roof instead.

As we get closer to Tauranga, we get signal for the phone and we call our families to let them know where we are and that we are safe. Phil's family is very happy to hear from him. They were worried. I can hear the relief in their voice when he calls.

I ring my boys and two of them say 'Oh, are you on the boat now? I didn't know.' My single boys, wrapped up in their own world. I might be lost at sea and they wouldn't know for weeks.

It is my own fault I suppose. For at least two years, I was off on my motorbike, house sitting in a new suburb every month. Not even close family could be expected to remember where I was in those days. Coombabah? Tarragindi? No that was last month. If I didn't have a mobile phone, even Phil would have lost touch with me.

Just before dusk, we get ready for the night. The sails are going great guns and we are speeding along at six knots, so Phil leaves them up. It is about jogging speed for a fit person, but in the dark it feels as if we are flying. We see the lights of a large cargo ship near the shore, but after watching it for some time and checking the radar, we are confident it is stopped.

A few minutes later, the big ship begins to move. It crosses from our left to our right and sets up for what looks like the shipping channel that we want to use. A small boat arrives to guide it in. Phil slows and decides to put down the sails so he has more control. We are at least two nautical miles away, but in the dark it looks closer and neither of us wants to take a chance.

For the rest of the way, we creep in at 3 knots and it takes such a long time. It is already almost midnight and we are so tired. Watching out in the dark is tiring, but Phil has the worst of it. He has better eyes in the dark, so I am just a backup.

I spend ages watching the moonlight on the water. When I was young, I used to feel special because the moon seemed to follow me when I was in the car. Now, I have that same sense of grandeur. The moon is so far away, but it spreads light like a cosmic blanket over the water, and it leads straight to me. The stars are so clear and pretty, and there are still finger wisps of cloud along the skyline.

I begin to feel like a secret agent spy or something, creeping into port after dark. Just a few weeks ago, we were just regular middle-aged people, going for walks, and working in the garden. A big night out was fish and chips or a six o'clock movie and we went to bed as soon after 8.30 pm as we could. Now we are out at midnight, steering a boat into port through the starry blackness. And this is the second time in a week.

Phil seems so much younger on this trip, He is enthusiastic and happy, even in a crisis he is calm. I have loved seeing him cope with one problem after the other and get us through the tough times. When he is standing on the roof of our cabin, being thrown up and down as he fixes the sails, or furls a rope, I fall in love with him all over again. I feel so safe to have him here, making it all happen no matter what.

Tonight is no different. We change over and I steer as he guides us quietly into the harbour channel and across to a spot he has chosen before coming here. There are quite a few boats here already and we need to weave around some before we find just the right spot. Phil lets down the noisy anchor, I turn off the noisy engine, and everyone can rest.

Tonight, there will be no night watch and I don't need to sleep on the claustrophobic side of the bed because Phil shouldn't need to get out of bed.

No engine noses. No flapping sails. No risk of running into a tanker or a fishing boat. Just the small concern about making sure our anchor holds and we do not drift into anyone else. After the last few nights, not much at all.

# Stuck in Tauranga

Phil got up once in the night to check that we hadn't drifted into the city, but mostly it was a quiet night. After the late bedtime, I am happy to stay in bed and read a book, but Phil is up. He is trying to fix the inverter so we will have a computer, and be able to use the navigation program.

I eat the last two banged up apples left from Napier while Phil calls the marina to get us a spot for the day. He also calls the sailmaker and there is no answer.

As usual, it takes us most of an hour, just to get across the bay to a marina we could see from where we were anchored.

The visitor berth is at the end of the marina and there is a four-day camel march between boats to the marina. As we walk, I look at the boats and their names. I wonder if the superyacht owners look down on people like us on our steel and rust ocean caravans.

It is a long way to the end, so I amuse myself by reading boat names. I like 'Aquasition,' 'Game Boy,' 'Reel Addiction,' and my favourite 'Seas the Day'. 'Purrfect' looks familiar and might have been in Napier when we were there.

At the marina office, while Phil explains our situation, I study the pictures on the noticeboard. They have a super collection of stranded and damaged boats. One yacht is sitting on top of a rock, balanced perfectly on its keel. It must have hit at high tide, and then it became a high-rise sculpture at low tide.

Another picture shows a marina with all the boats piled up against each other. Scores of them. I think it happened in north Australia after a cyclone had lifted all the boats off their moorings.

It doesn't seem designed to inspire confidence. The lady is lovely though. We get several books of yacht information and she solves the mystery of the unresponsive sailmaker. She makes a few calls and finds out that he is having his first day off in a very long time. Great timing for us, especially as he is the only sailmaker in Tauranga now.

We ask about fuel. We want to fill up the diesel tank as we have done so much motoring and seem to be destined to do more. The receptionist isn't sure if there is any fuel in their pump. We will have to go to the pump and see.

Back on the yacht I make a bang-up breakfast of readymade beans, bangers, and bacon, along with instant mashed potato, eggs, and a tomato, the only fresh thing left on the boat.

While we are eating, we can see the fuel pump and notice some men getting fuel for their boat. They seem to be successful so we untie our boat and head across to get some for ourselves.

There is fuel in the pump but there is another problem. We have to pay at the machine first and the machine will not work for me. I try again and again with both my New Zealand cards. The previous people managed to get their fuel; I don't know what I am doing wrong. After I have tried at least twenty times, I give up and call the service number on the machine. The lady on the phone tells me the Internet connection is down and they will send out a serviceman.

I suspect that won't be any time soon.

We stay a few minutes to fill up our water tank and I am astounded to see a repair man arrive just minutes after my call. We decide to wait for him to fix it since we are already here.

It is one o'clock and frustrating that we haven't achieved much, but it is a serene and scenic place to wait. We have blue sky, expensive looking boats, picture perfect clouds and a fabulous view across the bay to Mount Maunganui. Who can complain?

On the rock wall nearby, are a dozen gannets preening on the rocks, while others are floating in the water or diving for fish. They remind me of the gannets we saw in China, only these ones are not attached to a Chinese fisherman by a string that circles their necks so they cannot swallow the fish they catch. These are wild birds.

It is nice to watch them freely come and go, their legs making little plops on the water as they take off. There are other birds too. Seagulls with their insistent calls, and a large white and yellow gull, lumbering across the water on take-off as if he is the 747 of the bird world.

A lady in a kayak comes by, following a man swimming in scuba gear. The water is just a few feet deep and I am curious. She says he is checking for sea creatures that would be hazardous to the marina. She says it is a much better place to be than in an office. I couldn't agree more.

We wait there for about half an hour but eventually, the technician tells us it is a modem problem that he can't fix easily. He has to give up, and so do we.

We motor back to the visitor dock and make the long trek down to the marina office. This time we take our rubbish down to the bins. The office lady said it would be okay to leave our rubbish here, but not to let anyone know. I am not sure how we can make it look less obvious when we are carrying our bags of our trash. We have all the smaller bags in one large black bag. Perhaps people will think it is our laundry or something.

I just hope any residual flies are suffocated by the spray I put in the bags, or at least well contained. I don't want to be responsible for bringing a new colony of highly fertile flies to the port.

Now we still need to get fuel. At least we have another option.

There is a pump at a second marina further up the nearby river. We spend the early afternoon getting there and then negotiate the turns carefully. There are a lot of expensive boats here too.

Phil steers us gently into the fuel dock, wedged at the end of a row of boats, and adjacent to a nearby tributary. There is a strong current from an incoming tide which helps push the boat into the edge of the wharf. The boat is now pinned against the dock by the current and Phil begins wondering how he will be able to get away.

Everything at this pump works, so we fill up with fuel. While we are there the sailmaker rings back. He says he is working a half day, but I suspect he is being kind. We called three times, left one message, and the marina office also called on our behalf. He probably guessed we were desperate.

He offers to pick up the sail from the fuel dock and is there before we have loaded all our fuel. He quotes us only $5 more than the upholsterer in Gisborne charged and it is now a much longer rip and will need more work.

We decide to stay in the marina for the night to make it easier for the sailmaker, and because we need a new cord to charge our computer. I go to the office while Phil does some thinking about how to get the boat off the dock.

The people in the office are even friendlier than at the last marina. They tell me that we should stay at the fuel pump until 6 pm when the tide will change. I am amazed. Who planned a fuel pump that you could only enter or leave when the tide was in the right direction?

At least we have a few hours to spare to visit town.

The office lady explains that we can walk into town, or walk the other way and catch a bus to a suburban mall. We decide to catch a bus.

It turns out to be a very long walk to the bus stop. By the time the first bus arrives, we are hot and tired. It is not going to the mall, but we get on anyway. It is going to Mount Maunganui but I am sure we can find a way back from there. I don't want to wait any longer in the hot sun.

Mount Maunganui is a pleasant strip of shops that seem very holiday centred. Behind it is the large hill that looks out to sea and gives the suburb its name. We don't have time for this big hill, but we climb a small one and are rewarded by views that look right across the ocean towards White Island in one direction, and into the bay where we stayed last night in the other.

Because we can, we buy drinks and ice cream. Even our diet is on holiday ... again.

We have no trouble getting a bus to take us back but we still face a long walk. Our bus will drive right past the marina but there is no place to park and so the closest bus stop is the one where we have to walk a long way. Our only other option is to go all the way into town in the other direction.

As we get back, tired and hot, it is only minutes after the appointed high tide time. There is someone standing on the wharf by our boat and we are surprised to see Dave from the boat Desolina. He tells us that he and Ruth didn't plan to stop in here anymore than we did.

We tell him about our ripped sail and computer trouble, and he tells us about their engine troubles. Theirs is a much more modern looking sleek and speedy yacht, but it seems every boat has its problems.

At least being in a marina we have a chance to do some washing and have hot showers. We also decide to have dinner at the restaurant attached to the marina. We feel we have to try it, especially when we see that it is called 'Phil's Place.'

We sit looking out over the marina and share a rich seafood chowder, pork belly, lamb chops, and a plate of seasonal vegetables. Occasionally, small commercial planes fly low overhead on their way to land at the airport behind us, and boats sway gently in their moorings.

We watch a yacht similar to ours come in with a canoe and a surfboard tied to it. The only crew member is wearing a ripped shirt and grubby shorts.

'Our kind of yachty,' says Phil. 'but he has more toys than us.'

I laugh. 'We have more than he does. I bet he doesn't have surface rust, dodgy electrics, and a ripped sail.'

'Or a rusty metal sculpture tied to the railing,' adds Phil. The part of our davit that fell off in rough sea, is now tied to the railing alongside the ripped life preserver Phil once suggested 'might not be able to save itself in high seas, let alone one of us'. It is so old and ripped that it might possibly dissolve in water and fizz up like Alka-Seltzer.

We love our boat, we really do. It was once on the cover of a magazine about cruising yachts, but right now she could be the poster girl for yachts in distress. I look forward to seeing how she looks after Phil restores her.

This is the relaxing side of yachting. Visiting new places and having dinner in beautiful restaurants. Phil reminds me that if we had more time, we would not be sailing in the harsh weather we have experienced. We would just wait until the wind and weather are in our favour.

While we are eating and talking, the sun sinks behind the clouds on the horizon. The sky explodes into a burst of flamingo pink and burnt orange with golden halos, and then slowly fades to silver and grey. Surely there is no more spectacular place to eat in all the world.

It is a very special night and the food is delicious. It is perfectly cooked and beautifully presented. We walk down the marina to bed, tired and very happy.

Three hours later, I can't sleep, so I sit looking out over the side of the boat. Three hours and five minutes later, all that delicious dinner comes back up and ends up floating in the river.

Sometimes I think of my friends who know I have gone sailing. I suspect they assume I am doing something much more glamourous.

# Tauranga City and Night Sailing

Since we left on this trip, we have changed our diet completely. At home, I like fresh squeezed juice and scrambled eggs for breakfast. Today I made pancakes because I was feeling empty, and that seemed like a good idea. Now I feel sick again.

On the boat, we have what will store well and be easy to cook. Along with all the packet foods, and canned meals, I bought two plastic bottles of pancake mix, and it turns out that each will make us three breakfasts. They are full of white flour and artificial flavours and colours, something I usually avoid at home. Next time I will bring more eggs, and maybe porridge.

The sail is being delivered this morning and we desperately need a computer cable to power our navigation program. Phil suggests I go to town for the cable while he stays to meet the sail maker. I have a better idea. I call a mobile computer repair specialist and he says he has the cable we need and will deliver it for $5. I feel very pleased with myself.

Since I don't have to go to town, Phil suggests I scrub the deck. I assume he is joking. Then he reminds me that when we were enjoying the view of White Island, we both got up with dark and gritty marks on our clothes. I suppose I could have thought of that before.

Cleaning the deck turns out to be satisfying. The anti-slip pads on our deck, change from grubby black to a less grubby grey. It is the best we can expect on a boat of this age.

At the appointed time, we down our tools and go to meet the computer guy. He is early and is already sitting at the table where we arranged to meet, the cable next to his elbow. I am astounded and disappointed. He has brought the wrong cable. I asked for a figure eight cable. He has brought a cable that has three prongs at the end and looks more like part of the Olympic rings than a figure eight. He says it is the new version.

Phil says he might have to adapt it if we can't find the proper cable and so we agree to buy it, but I have to go to town. We ask the man if he is going that way and if he will drop us off.

Phil asks me if I want him to come too, and I say yes. He has lots to do and would much rather stay and do it, but I am not sure I want to be with the computer man alone. Plus, it might be fun to look around town together.

When the computer guy drops us off, I need to give him some money for the cord and a little more for the petrol would be good. I am not sure what to offer him. I only have $5 which is probably too little and $20 which I think is too much.

I give both notes to Phil so he can decide and he gives both to the driver who accepts. I am astounded. A taxi would have cost us less. A nicer person would have dropped us off for free. He was going that way anyway.

Phil is astounded too. 'Why did you give it to me then?' he says. Sometimes I forget he can't read my mind.

The driver says he has business at the same electronics store that we stop at and he follows us in. I think maybe he has pegged us for big spenders and thinks there might be a way to get more money from us. I am relieved when we have to move to another store and he doesn't follow.

It takes us three more stores to find what we are looking for. Phil is in a desperate hurry to get back and I feel bad for asking him to come. I didn't want to see town without him. Now I am not seeing town with him. We charge around looking for a taxi stand or a bus stop, whatever will get us back faster.

I feel about as bad as I have felt on this trip. I could have had a lovely morning if I had been sensible enough to let Phil stay and do what he needed to do.

When we finally get a bus, I ask the driver if he can drop us off at the marina. I know there is no bus stop there, but the bus goes right past and I don't want to walk as far as we did yesterday.

The bus driver gives me a perfectly reasonable five-minute explanation about how an unscheduled stop could cause an accident, or complaints from other passengers, or worse. As we sit down Phil notices that I am not happy. He asks if I am alright. 'Not really,' I say, and tears start down my face. It is not just the walk we have ahead of us, but the time we have wasted on this errand. I insisted Phil come and he isn't having any fun.

Phil puts an arm around me and I feel even worse because I can't stop the tears. I was up a bit last night so perhaps lack of sleep is part of my melt down.

Suddenly the bus stops, and Phil is halfway to the door. The bus driver has stopped at the marina after all and so I run down the aisle to catch up. Calling out our thanks, we walk back to our boat in silence. Phil is concerned, but all I can say is that I am not really turning into weepy-woman. I am just tired and out of sorts. The bus driver's kindness has made me feel worse. He must have seen me upset and now I feel silly, crying over having to walk.

The bus trip wasn't even that long. I wonder if we could have walked to town in the same amount of time that it took us to walk to the bus stop in the other direction.

At the boat, I charge the computer with our new and expensive computer cable, and then check emails and get our wind prediction files. I have a quick lie down but then I remember that I was in the middle of cleaning the deck when we left, and go out to finish it.

When Phil has finished with the engine, and I have had a enough cleaning, we take the marina key back to the office and stop at the café on the way back. Phil is being especially nice and offers to stop for lunch before we go.

I buy sandwiches, and rice and vegetable rolls, and a passionfruit and mango smoothie. I also get some warm bread and dips from the restaurant from last night. Other people ordered them and they looked so good. Phil gets a burger. Just in case we do not have enough, I get another smoothie to take away and Phil gets a mango and coconut slice.

We take most of it back to the boat and get ready to leave. I am not excited about getting back onto the bumpy ocean. That may explain the extended visit to the café and the huge stock up of comfort food. Tauranga has been a nice stopover and we have met some nice people here.

If we had more time, I would have liked to climb the stately Mount Maunganui hill overlooking the harbour, and visit some of the beaches here. I look forward to the day when we can stay as long as we want in any port.

Only three hours later than we planned, we head out.

It takes us an hour to cross the bay, but I like watching the city skyline and the green hills around the shores. In between setting up the GPS and steering while Phil works on something, I take close up photos of the port markers.

As we leave the protection of the sheltered bay, the ocean is less bumpy than it has been, and we seem to be running smoother. There is not much wind but for once we are running away from it, not into it. There is swell too, but it is a smoother ride. I can stand in the middle of the floor, and balance without holding on. It is also nice to go to the toilet without needing a crash helmet and knee and elbow guards.

It has been two hours since we left but Tauranga seems as if it is still just a short walk away. 'Is it too late to order KFC?' asks Phil. 'If we call out, do you think they would lob us a chicken thigh and a tub of coleslaw?'

The sunset tonight is all peach and apricot smudges over a silver-grey horizon. In the East there are echoes of soft pink along the clouds. I take some photos, but not many. After the stunning sunset at the restaurant the night before, this is tame.

Just after dark, we pass Mayor Island. We had talked about visiting there but have now decided to head directly for Great Barrier Island. If the wind keeps up, we could get there by 3 pm tomorrow and if not, then we will be there in the middle of the night as usual.

We are still sailing along slowly. The wind is not strong enough to push us fast. It seems as if we spend all our time getting places. We are so slow that I sometimes expect to see seagulls floating past us. I think the reason the dolphins like us is because we give them a chance to relax and swim slowly. They probably leave when they are tired of going at the equivalent of crawling speed for a dolphin.

Eventually the sun goes down, exploding into orange that turns the clouds into a watercolour portrait of orange sand dunes, washing the edges of the sky.

A big tanker comes up behind us. We put on more lights so we have less chance of being collected by a ship built like a multi-story building lying on its side. I hope it is not a cruise liner. We are only a few steps up from a bathtub with a sail. The idea of passengers leaning on their shuffleboard mallets or peering over their evening cocktails at our little steel tub in the ocean is not an appealing thought.

In the marina, someone told me that our boat looks as if it would be good in heavy weather. I think it is because it looks like it is already bogged down deep in the water. It is so low to the ocean that it seems to be already hunkered down into the wind. Everyone else seems to have decks much higher above the water. We look as if we are already in the process of sinking.

We both watch the big ship nervously. It is early evening. They are probably already be on autopilot and not watching. I have a question for Phil.

'Big ships must have really good processes for making sure they don't run into anyone. Even if they are not worried about hitting us, they would hate a delay in their schedule that would follow. And there must be a lot of paperwork. Wouldn't that make them more careful?'

Phil says 'hitting us would just be a way of getting barnacles off the bottom of their ship. They might not even notice.'

I sit up straighter and watch their movements more closely. 'It must be time to tack,' I say.

Phil looks confused.

'When there is a dangerous tanker nearby, don't we usually tack into their path?' I don't think Phil found that as funny as I expected.

When the ship has disappeared over the horizon ahead of us, Phil takes the opportunity to get some sleep. The radar is on and the autopilot is steering us, so I don't need to do anything. I decide to watch one of the movies that I stored on my computer for just this sort of night. It turns out to be very arty, with odd story lines and lots of close-up shots of the back of the main character's head as she walks, but it passes the time.

As it finishes, I realise I have run the computer down to ten percent and we will need it again to navigate. I plug it in to charge, and the inverter squeals as if it is being strangled with its own cord. I hope it is not the new cord we just bought.

I keep trying to get the charger working because we need this computer for navigation. Inevitably, the noise wakes my poor tired husband. After a quick check of the electrical system, he decides the house battery is too low to charge the computer properly. There is no sun to charge the solar panels at this time of night and the wind is not strong enough to spin the wind generator. Phil has no choice but to start the engine just so we can have some power for our computer.

It is 11 pm at night. I was hoping to enjoy the peace a bit longer.

Before he can start the motor, he has to grease something and then he has to change the fan belt. He was hoping to put it off until morning, but now he knows it can't wait. Back he goes into the bilge. What a way to start the night.

# Dolphins and Potholes in the Ocean

It is a hard night.

I am awake for some of it but, as usual, Phil is up and down for most of it. The motor is happily churning away, but sometime in the night, it gets into my brain. I find myself wide awake and unable to block out the cacophony coming from the pounding of the engine. I ask Phil if he can turn it off.

He is a thoughtful person, so he does. Then the sails start their flapping, and banging, and carrying on and it is just a different kind of noise. It is also a noise that suggests the sails are in danger of slashing themselves into large rags. Phil has to get back up and turn on the engine and we just have to deal with it.

The waves wash in from the open ocean all night and there is not much wind. We are rolling and the kitchen equipment is rolling and I could really, really, really do without the rolling.

At dawn, I wake feeling somewhat sorry for myself yet again. The engine is pounding out like a hundred jungle drums, the bed is uncomfortable and the sheets are the wrong shape and size for it. The quilt is too hot and the air too cold and there is not enough space ... and on and on.

I worry about myself and then I remember it is worse for Phil. He hasn't been able to relax all night.

He is out there right now and adjusting the sails which are still slapping around in the too light wind. I get up reluctantly, because I need to be there in case he falls over the side or something. As I put one foot out on deck, I spot a flash of silver in the water. I am cheered to see a dolphin. But is it a dolphin?

The water is still dark and the early morning light too slanted to see clearly. I wonder whether sharks look the same as dolphins when they swim. I watch their slick shiny steel grey backs as several curve out of the water, dorsal fins proud and then I notice the white undersides. Our ocean companions are sloughing alongside, doing tricks like kids in a skateboard race. They are definitely dolphins and not ocean killers.

I am intrigued with the difference between this sunrise and the sunset I saw last night. The sun looks a little different coming than it does going. This morning it is less flaming orange and more shining yellow buttery gold. Less like the bright yolk of the fresh eggs we get from our own chickens and more like the anaemic yellow yoke of a commercial egg.

When the dolphins leave, I press myself back into the corner of the seat to counteract the rolling of the waves. They are still coming side on and trying to toss me all over the place. This is one of those mornings when even getting to the toilet is a challenge and staying on it almost impossible. The lid keeps falling onto my back.

Getting back from the bathroom involves bursting through the door no matter how gentle I try to be, and then grabbing whatever is in reach, then probably still falling sideways. Hopefully onto the couch.

At least the carpet is not all bunched up to one side again like it was last time. I have removed it completely.

I sit down to write and find it best to sit sideways, braced by both legs on two different surfaces. That way the paper doesn't fall from side to side but up and down with me.

As I write I must look worried. Phil asks if I am writing a note to place in a bottle asking for a rescue. It is tempting.

82

This is one of those days when you spend your time holding on and don't try anything tricky, like washing dishes or cooking. I spend most of my time trying to keep bruising to a minimum. I eliminate trips to get anything less important than water, or my camera. I don't open any cupboards, and don't make any sudden moves. I am glad I had the forethought to pack muesli bars and other snacks but I'm not sure if I have the stomach to eat them anyway. I'm not feeling seasick but I still have a tender tummy.

I enjoy the scenery this morning, but only in short bursts. One moment I can see the whole ocean on one side, including water that should be under our boat, and then the boat flips back up and blocks my view of low-lying clouds. Then another flip and the window is almost where the floor should be.

I have been hoping to visit a place called 'Hole in the Wall'. I find it on the map, and calculate it is half an hour away at our blistering speed of 3 knots, a slow walking speed. I will need all that time to get my contact lenses into my eyes without blinding myself.

Phil and I laugh about how much I intend to do this morning. My list is;

1. Get dressed
2. Put lenses in and
3. Make the bed (optional)

First, I dress and it has the coordination of a circus balancing act. I lean back and put one leg in my pants. Lean forward and put on one flip flop. Lean back and try to rebalance myself and miss. Lean forward and fall onto the bedroom shelf, hands first. Lean back and put the other leg in my pants, lean forward and stand up, lean back and pull my pants up. Etc. etc.

One day it will all flow better and I won't need to rebalance or fall against any furniture, but I have already come a long way. A week ago, this routine included a head butt into the cupboards and a bounce back to the wall.

Making the bed is more a matter of bracing myself and waiting for the part I want to make, to come to me.

Phil is impressed that I managed it on several counts.

1. Degree of difficulty
2. The sheets and quilt have been spun around by two people who were up and down all night and
3. The bed is musty because I have been hot and restless and we still can't find the missing deodorant.

It is also significant that after half the night in the box part of the bed with the low roof, the air got thin and I felt claustrophobic. I insisted Phil swap sides so I could sleep on the outside. He had to spend the second half of the night climbing over me every time he got up to check the horizon.

After I have done everything on my list except my lenses, the rest of the morning is more relaxing. As relaxing as a ride on a bucking fairground ride can be.

I check the map and find we are going to arrive at Great Barrier Island about midnight as per usual. I relock the cupboard door into place so it stops banging, I catch a sliding water bottle, and look for tankers on the horizon. Several times I also refit the non-slip mat that has slipped onto the floor again.

It is almost lunchtime when I get the courage to put my contact lenses into my eyes.

Yesterday I nearly lost one as it slipped off my finger and into the sink. On our first day at sea, I took all day to get them in. With that and all the boat motion and the sea-sickness, everything was blurry all day. Today is an accomplishment as I get them in my eyes quickly and with only a few tears.

Phil cuts up the sandwich we got from the café in Tauranga and we have very acceptable breakfast, if not traditional. It is beef with cheese, salad, and coleslaw. I don't believe I ever had coleslaw for breakfast before. It isn't bad. Plus, it stays down. Score one for my love of food and none for sea-sickness.

I am not sure how Phil does it, but he showers and heads off to bed for some badly needed sleep. The sea has calmed a little but I am not game enough to attempt a shower myself. I need both hands for balance today. Maybe I will have one when we come into a harbour. Besides I am worn out with dressing myself and making the bed.

The coastline here alongside New Zealand's Coromandel Peninsular, is beautiful. Craggy and new looking, as if it has not been worn down yet by the sea. There are many small islands here and some are just jagged lumps in the ocean. Steep sided like upside down pots with scraped down sides, or pointy like shark teeth.

Most have dark green foliage for hair, blank rock faces, and skirts of dark brown where the ocean has worn away the lower levels. There are rounded hills further away, and the nearby land mass seems to be cream and rust cliffs topped with pine tree forests; probably destined for export.

The whole area looks fresh, and young. Unmoulded by time. Wild and new.

We come across a little chocolate and cream coloured bird floating all alone in the water like a slightly large duckling. Shortly after that, we sail past flocks of the same birds, sociable together but obviously less psychically connected than most birds seem to be. As we approach, they fly away in several different directions until the smaller groups gradually reroute themselves and follow the larger groups and they gather again somewhere else.

While Phil sleeps, I get the computer to myself and a chance to transcribe the handwritten notes I have been keeping to document the trip. I want to copy them while I still remember everything clearly because the handwriting is all wobbly from writing while the boat lurches.

I copy half a day and six notebook pages. That is quite an accomplishment even though the sea has calmed some. Now it is time to take a break and maybe watch a movie. Or maybe take that shower. So much to do.

According to our navigation program, we have forty nautical miles to go and we are doing almost four knots. I have plenty of time to spare. Phil is now up and awake. I should continue to write or do something else useful but instead I decide to have a sleep.

Two hours later, Phil tells me how long I have been in bed and I am surprised. I feel as if I was awake the whole time.

During my rest, I heard Phil's voice say my name. I knew it was inside my head, but I got up anyway. When I told Phil, he said he had the same thing happen to him. He heard me say his name and then looked around and I was asleep. I am not sure what to make of that but it sure seems weird.

I wonder if I have bought too many spicy foods with us.

It is 3.15 in the afternoon and I feel like some tomato soup for lunch. Yes lunch. During this trip, time has become a fluid thing. We eat when we are hungry and sometimes, we even miss meals, especially when the deck is churning beneath us as it is today. We are much more guided by appetite than we are at home.

Phil is eating his emergency chicken chippies and offers me some, but I am a dedicated wife and even in this weather that is not a suitable lunch. A pre-lunch snack? Yes, of course. But I have my heart set on tomato soup.

Unluckily, the only soup we have a mysterious Laksa soup that is full of mushrooms and tofu. It is also neon yellow as if it is a chunky yellow paint. I decide not to inflict it on Phil, he deserves better.

I decide to make him some chicken and corn noodles. Less healthy, but less likely to come back up. The boat is still unsteady and is back to the lurching roll it had this morning but I feel confident I can do it this time.

The stove is swinging back and forth but the saucepan of water heats nicely, so I drop in the soup pouch. It swings sedately back and forth, but it stays in the pan.

When the soup pouch is warm, I take it out, snip the corner, and put it into a bowl. I put the bowl down on the bench and refill the pot with water to start Phil's not-so-gourmet noodles.

In the ten seconds the bowl is unsupervised, it takes on a life of its own and scoots across the bench, flinging yellow curry soup over a plastic container and the salt and pepper shakers. It even severs the head off a plastic spoon on the way.

I look around in despair. What a disaster. There is soup left in the bowl but much more of it is smeared over the condiments and making yellow trails down the kitchen wall.

It is a tribute to my determination, that it only takes me ten minutes to clean it up with paper towels, clean out the saucepan, heat up some fresh water, and make Phil's noodles.

It won't be the world's cleanest bench, but it is the sort of thing that can wait until we get to a stable parking spot and be done more thoroughly. Maybe.

We arrive at Great Barrier Island with just enough time to find our bay and anchor before it gets too dark to see. There is a narrow passage we have to negotiate but it is much wider than it looks on the map. Past that, we have a choice of calm and sheltered bays, and we have chosen to stay in the one we read about in a yachting magazine.

At Smokehouse Bay there is a corrugated iron cabin and clothes washing facilities such as concrete tubs and rotating lines, a shower, a shed to smoke fish in, and best of all, a bath that is fed with water from a stream high above. All we need to do is to collect firewood and light a fire to have hot water.

It is exciting when we arrive at our destination. It has been a year since we read the article, and this is a dream come true for us.

After we have made a lot of noise setting the anchor, and hoping we haven't annoyed the neighbours too much, we plan to fish for our dinner, but then we change our minds.

Neither of us wants to kill and gut a fish tonight. Or maybe ever. We have spent far too long as city dwellers and the idea of killing anything, even a cold-blooded fish, makes both of us cringe.

We decide to stick to our beef with red wine and mashed potato, followed by chocolate pudding and white sauce. Not too shabby for a 5-minute instant meal out in one of New Zealand's most gorgeous and hidden spots.

Looking across this huge shining inlet, it looks as serene as a lake. It is surrounded on all sides by lush green hills as if it is a hidden world known only by a few intrepid travellers like us. There is only one yacht in our bay, but there are other yachts in some of the bays across the way, their little mast lights shining weakly. It is so quiet and peaceful, punctuated with little plips of birds diving for fish, or fish doing whatever they do that sends up bubbles and ripples from the depths of a placid ocean bay.

It almost seems obscene to consider catching fish here.

Phil and I clean up and head to bed early, hoping for a quiet night. The boat is barely moving and I feel unbalanced by the stillness and the lack of movement. I hope I can sleep. Tonight, we will not need to change the sails, work on the motor, check the heading, or scan the horizon for approaching ships. It will be a nice change.

# Smokehouse Bay

We have woken up in paradise. Molten metal coloured water, framed by dark green hills covered in trees with twisted grey trunks and bushy tops. Behind and above, are neat rows of dark pine trees that have been planted for timber. It is so quiet. I can hear every little fish splash and bird call.

Schools of fish occasionally surface, thrashing the water into spurting foam. Birds pass, calling to each other in mournful tones. Cicadas start up their summer chorus and are done by mid-morning. In between, it is still and isolated, wonderland quiet.

This place is enchanting and I am glad we get to stay here. Whether we stay for longer depends on the weather report that Phil has requested to be emailed to us. I don't want to admit it to Phil, but I hope the weather for a Tasman crossing is bad enough that we can relax and spend more time exploring this area.

We have to be back in Brisbane for the end of the month because Phil is due back at work soon after. If we don't get good weather, we can stay sailing in the area for a little longer.

After a relaxing breakfast of porridge with peach puree, the neighbours call by in their dinghy. Steve and Heidi are interesting and very realistic about cruising. They have been doing it for ten years now and been as far as Fiji. They are older than us, and although we don't ask, we assume they are retired.

89

'That could be us one day,' says Phil.

I sure hope so. All day to go nowhere. I am already getting used to taking all day just to do dishes and get dressed.

There is no wharf here, so unless we swim to the island, we will have to blow up the expensive dinghy we bought before we came. It has a foot powered pump so I expect it to take most of the morning ... but it doesn't.

It is very efficient and Phil has it done by the time I have made milo and marmite crackers for morning tea. (Yes, we did just have breakfast, but it was a late breakfast.)

Now for our first shore trip in the little boat we decide to call Mini Manuka.

Phil gets in first and carefully lifts in the small but heavy outboard. It came with the yacht and we have not used it before. Once it is fitted to the transom, Phil pulls the ripcord and is almost sent flying when it doesn't start. It is not far to shore so he decides to row and I get in.

At least some of me does.

The bag I have over my shoulder catches on the boat rail and I am stuck halfway off the boat with the strap around my neck. Phil reaches over, and between us we get me free and into the front of the boat. Another undignified entrance.

While I lounge around in the front pretending to be Lady Muck, Phil rows us to shore. The couple we met before are there and we have a lovely time just exploring and talking.

There are seats and a table under some magnificent big trees. To the left is a tin shed with the famous bath in it and to the right, the tubs, and clothes hoists that are already filled with our new friends' washing.

It is only a small sandy area, and behind it the hill rises steeply. It seems like a quiet place now, but there is a notice board that hints of a wild nightlife that sometimes takes place here.

After chatting with the couple for a few minutes, mostly about how much yachting costs, and how much we have spent on our respective yachts, another couple arrives. They have some fish and are here to smoke them.

We ask them about the walk across the island, but although they have been here several times, they have never done it.

'An American man got lost up there the other day,' says Steve, in a way that makes it sound as if he is still up there somewhere, probably walking in circles and looking for a way out.

'How hard can it be?' I wonder. It is a narrow neck of land with a bay on the other side. Where could you go except down to the water? We decide to follow the track ourselves and head off up along the path into the bush.

Near the top, I notice some large animal droppings on the path.

'There are horses up here,' I say.

'Those are cow pats,' says Phil, and minutes later a rather large black and white bull appears and confirms it.

It is big and scary, and I am poised to run, but it turns and heads off into the bush, crashing through small tree branches and stumbling over roots. I watch it go with relief and then I search for a suitably large sharp stick and carry it for the next little while.

At the other end of the path, we emerge through a thicket of trees and past a small rippling stream onto a secluded beach. The tide is out and the ground is covered in small open pipi shells, and oyster shells. Too bad they are empty. Shellfish might have been a nice option since we have yet to be brave enough to catch and kill a fish.

There are no signs of anyone here except for a hanging rope and little stick swing. Phil and I dare each other to sit on it, just for fun. Secluded is good, when you are two fifty somethings acting like five-year-olds.

As we return to Smokehouse Bay, I remind Phil that the couple we met told us how an American man got lost up here.

'It is so hard to get lost,' I say as I forge ahead. 'There are pieces of blue rope tied to trees at intervals along the way and it is easy to follow.'

Perhaps that is when I take my eyes off the path, because two minutes later, the bush around us begins to look unfamiliar. Somewhere along the way we have left the path we came in on. I laugh and Phil probably rolls his eyes and wonders why he let me lead.

We decide to carry on down the increasingly steep slope and soon we can see the bay and the smokehouse, so we just keep going until we meet up with the path again.

'See,' I say. 'Easy.'

We return to our boat in Mini Manuka, me lying lazily in the back again as Phil rows us back. It is a compact boat, and I wriggle around trying to find a position for my legs so they are not in the way when Phil works the oars.

It is a warm day and the walk has made me hot, so although there is a slight breeze, I decide to go swimming. I get dressed and then collect my mask, snorkel and flippers.

With no small amount of effort, I manage the flippers around the rungs of our ladder and then fall backwards into the water. As elegant as ever.

It is cool alright, but I keep telling Phil how lovely and warm it is while he keeps asking if there are ice bergs.

I lived in New Zealand for most of my life and find this perfectly acceptable weather to swim, but Phil has lived mainly in Australia where the water is warmer. He has no desire to join me but gets tired of me teasing him about being chicken and decides to get in.

He strips to his undies and starts to climb down. It takes him even longer to get in than it did me, and all the time he is on the ladder, I wonder if our friends on shore can see that his waistband says BONDS in large letters. I don't think he expected to swim in New Zealand at all, even though it is just past the middle of summer.

He once swam in a hole in the Antarctic in midwinter and he learned to scuba dive in New Zealand's coldest region, sometimes on freezing cold nights, but times have changed. When he jumps in, he is out again within half a minute. 'Do you call that warm?' he says.

I laugh at him as I float easily in the water. I am comfortable enough now that I am used to the temperature, but I have my knees tucked up so my legs will not be eaten by anything lurking underneath.

I did look to see if there was anything in the water below, but it was just a sage green wall. Phil says he could see the boat keel from Mini Manuka, so I look again and realise that it is quite clear for at least thirty feet. There is just nothing at all to see. Good news for me I guess, but I figure it is time to get out anyway. The water here is deep. Who knows what is lurking beneath?

Later, after a lunch of packaged risotto, flavoured with chicken, pineapple and toasted cashews on top, we settle down for a nap. It doesn't last long. Some blowfly has got itself stuck on our yacht and keeps buzzing into the rear cabin where we were hoping to be sleeping. It does its zigzag rounds a few times and then heads out again. I read for a while then get up to write for a while. I could get that fly if only it would keep still for a few seconds.

After writing for some time and fly chasing for some time, I finally corner the fly down the back. As I spray it, it flies out the front hatch. I listen to it fly around the yacht and come back into the main cabin for another go. I follow it to our tiny bathroom and spray it well before locking it in. Unbelievably, I hear buzzing around the deck again but this time I am not sure. It might be in my head.

After our fly plague of a few days ago, I am much more aware of flies. Our rubbish is being locked away in the rear hatch every day or as soon as there is food in it but I don't want to take any chances. If there is anything organic, I drop it in the ocean.

This morning, I have a leftover rice, chicken and vegetable roll. I toss it overboard and it floats whole towards the neighbours' yacht, in one white ugly sodden lump. Embarrassed, I grab the boat hook to break it up. Suddenly fish appear in a feeding frenzy.

The lump begins to break up and soon it is just a white shape a few feet down, with fish circling it, and a small flotilla of shredded cabbage and carrot, still heading for the neighbours' yacht.

When Phil wakes up, I decide I want to fish. Phil and I hover over the huge cache of fishing gear I got at the Warehouse. Hooks of all sizes, pink and purple lures looking like sardines on ecstasy, red and white floats and sinkers in a myriad of shapes and sizes. Phil gets me a modest looking hook and I suggest it will only catch a tiny fish. He insists it will be a good size. Now what to use for bait?

I eye up the lures and choose a wiggly yellow bit of rubber. Phil thinks it is too big, so I figure we will never use them all and I sacrifice one by cutting into a more suitable size for the hook. It still wiggles. The fish will love it. And they do.

The line is down for a few seconds and something is biting. I pull up the line and a frustrated fish slides off the yellow rubbery thing. I put it down again and wait for something to happen. I have trouble sitting still, so within seconds, I pull the line in to check the length of line I am using and see how deep I am fishing. Just then I spot a brown rubbery lump on the deck about the size of a square pea.

I think it might be stray bit of tofu from last night. I might have tossed the last few rubbery pieces overboard and this is probably one that missed. I put it on the hook in front of the yellow wiggly thing. As soon as my hook sinks a little, something is biting my hook. Within a few more seconds I reel in a lovely creamy brown fish with purple flecks on the side and big accusing eyes.

'It is a Snapper,' say Phil. He is astounded. He was settling in to work on the small boat motor and assumed he had some time to work while I played at fishing. He was sort of hoping I wouldn't catch anything. Now someone has to kill and fillet our dinner.

Of course, it is Phil that has to do the dirty work and it seems to take a long time to stop twitching. I am fascinated as well as repulsed. We both apologise to the fish. With some difficulty, Phil guts it, removes the bones, and slices it into two small fillets, reducing it to a few slivers of edible meat.

'Shall I catch another?' I ask.

'Why not?' he says. I put a piece of our freshly caught fish on the hook and drop it in again.

Nothing happens - for all of thirty seconds. Then a minute later I am hauling a second Snapper over the side.

With no fridge, two fish are all we can use, so after Phil fillets the second fish, I head into the kitchen to prepare them. I decide to cook them simply, with a little salt, pepper, and a few garlic flakes. I serve it with instant cheesy mash and reconstituted dried peas. It is a nice feeling to be eating fish we cooked and prepared ourselves. I have a whole new love of cooking. Except for the instant mash. I might have had enough of that to last me a few years. I leave a bit on my plate and Phil quizzes me about it.

'I might put it on a hook and catch another fish,' I suggest.

'If you can use an old bit of tofu,' he says laughing, 'it might just work.'

After dinner, we are ready for another early night. There is a little rain and a soft mist settles over the area making it a new kind of beautiful. Phil turns on the engine to warm the water for our shower.

The engine is the only way we can heat our water at the moment and its loud thumping echoes between the hills.

'It's very noisy,' I say to Phil as if he hasn't noticed.

Phil suggest people are saying to each other 'It is late in the day for ploughing,' or 'where are they hiding a tractor in these hills?'

I think they are saying 'Good to see that old boat going. It is lowering the tone of the bay.'

Many more boats arrived during the day, and now there are about a dozen in this little bay. They are all going to be disappointed because we are not leaving. Just enjoying the sound of our engine. Hah.

Truthfully, everyone has been lovely, from the old couple on an old aluminium boat to the family on the new looking catamaran. I got a wave from them as they arrived. Nice people boaties, and there don't seem to be any pretentions. The old couple told me to expect it to cost big money and to be a lot of work, but that you would get your money back in sailing experiences. I like that philosophy and I believe it.

When the engine has been on for a minute, Phil heads for the shower. I am busily writing up notes about our adventures, but I stop because the boat seems to be moving. I go up to check and indeed we are moving ... in steady circles around the anchor.

'The boat seems to be moving,' I call out to Phil.

'Is the engine in gear?' he asks.

'The handle is straight up. I don't think so.'

He comes up and wiggles it some. It turns out it was in gear so he stops the engine. Yet more proof of my inability to work out anything on this yacht. Luckily the anchor seems to have held because there are about five other boats in bumping distance including the new and expensive looking catamaran with children on board.

Later, when we check the emails, there is good and bad news.

The weather report we requested says there are two possible problems with our trip to Australia. Both cyclones. It looks as if we won't be able to cross the Tasman Sea and I am so relieved. We can't stop in the middle of the ocean if the sail rips again. We won't be able to purchase parts for our electrics if we are way out to sea when the computer fails again. What if we run out of water? What if the engine stops or the mast falls off?

One thing this trip has taught me is that no matter how many backups you have, there is always something else that can go wrong.

The report is good news for me and bad news for Phil who has dreamed of this trip for years and was looking forward to working on our yacht in our own backyard.

I have to temper my enthusiasm for our new plans but I am quite happy that we can now do a bit more exploring in this area.


Phil and I settle down with a classic movie that we watch on our laptop in bed. Later, I wake to find Phil looking at me strangely.

'You are watching a movie with your eyes closed,' he says.

'Uh yes.' I roll over and turn off the computer so we can both get some sleep.

# Bathing in Public

Last night it rained but now this morning is cloudy and fine.

A large yacht is tied to the wooden posts near the Smokehouse Bay landing. It must have arrived early because the tide has gone out and the boat is now standing high and dry and balanced on its keel on muddy ground. The owners are underneath cleaning the hull, although it looks plenty clean to me.

Since we are not going to Australia, we need to make some new plans. We spend the whole morning scouring the Internet for somewhere to leave the yacht until we can come back next year. We contact several marinas and a few individuals and berths turn out to cost a minimum of twice what we were paying in Napier.

We consider hauling the boat out of the water and leaving it on dry land somewhere for a year, but that costs even more than a marina berth. The cheapest option would be to leave it moored to a buoy somewhere, but Phil is convinced that we will come back and find it completely empty, stripped by thieves.

As a last resort we contact a couple of people that do yacht deliveries. Phil would be disappointed not to make the crossing himself but I think it sounds like the best option. Then we get the quotes.

The first one wants seven thousand dollars.

The second one wants slightly less, but then we must pay for return airfares, food and living expenses – for three people. That will cost at least eight thousand dollars. It is not looking good.

Then I remember a man in Napier who told us he delivers yachts. He lives on a yacht and would probably love to spend two weeks sailing if we pay his expenses.

We track him down by calling the Napier marina. He sounds positive and asks for more information and photos. It takes the rest of the morning to write up all the details and take photos that show the yacht in a good light. He sends back an email. He can do it he says. It will cost twelve thousand dollars.

We politely decline and start looking for a marina that we can afford. Everything is so expensive. We decide to leave it for a few days.

Late in the morning, we head over to the bathhouse. We can see a little wreath of grey smoke, so we assume the fire is going and head over hoping for a hot bath.

A young couple has just finished. 'The bath is lovely,' The young man tells us. 'My wife had a bath in the outside tub.'

I look at the ratty old tub outside the shed and wonder why you would have a bath in the open and in full sight of several boats and their crew. There is another bath inside the hut. We plan to use that.

We fill the tub with hot water from the pipe that runs past the fireplace. There is plenty of water here. It comes from the little stream we passed earlier. Gravity feeds the water through pipes to both baths, a small group of wash tubs, and the hose. There are clotheslines too and over the morning they have filled up again with sheets, towels and clothes as people from nearby yachts bring over bags of washing.

I haven't had a bath in years. This leisurely pace is all part of the cruising yacht lifestyle. Some days it takes all day just to make lunch in a moving kitchen, and other days you spend hours just preparing for and having a relaxing bath. Nothing happens in a hurry when you are on a yacht.

I love having no appointments, no pressure, and no deadlines. I love having a bath in the middle of the day and having my husband home all day. I am not wild about having to sail in bad weather and rough seas, but I have to say it has been worth it.

Both of us are over fifty and looking forward to being retired. We just need to work out how to fund ourselves.

After our bath, we meet some of the other visitors to this bay. One couple has been here many times and tell us about a small village in a nearby bay. They say it has a shop and a bar, but not to bother with the bar because there is a stag party there this weekend.

We are expecting some high winds, and the village is protected from the worst weather so we decide to head there before it gets dark.

We arrived in Smokehouse Bay two days ago, and there was only one boat then. Now there are ten boats in our little bay, including two very large and expensive looking catamarans, sporting foreign flags.

This is going to be difficult.

Phil asks me to keep the boat in place as he takes up the anchor. I am nervous. Phil thinks the tide will drag us backwards and has asked me to be prepared to rev up the engine.

As he pulls up the anchor, I watch him carefully. He wants me to steer left, but of course the boat won't steer left without a bit of power. It is a big old boat and slow to respond at the best of times. When we are not moving, she will not turn at all.

I add some power and we are away. Phil points between some boats and I head in the suggested direction.

A man on one of the older yachts seems to be glaring at us as we pass. He looks as if he thinks we will run into him and I am relieved when we get past him.

I assume that the anchor is mostly up as I steer between the last two boats and out towards the bay.

The yacht with the grumpy man on it starts to follow us. As we continue through the yachts, he glides along behind us. I can't imagine why. Perhaps he thinks we will need some help. Perhaps he has seen that Phil struggled with the anchor. Every time I turn around, he is not far away and still glaring.

We are past all the other boats when Phil makes a discovery.

'Our anchor is caught and we are towing him along behind us,' he says.

I slow down and things get worse. His boat is still moving under its built-up momentum and is about to crash into us.

'Speed up,' says Phil.

I put on some power until we are far enough away to avoid a crash, but then we have to decide what to do. The grumpy man on the boat behind us is swearing his head off. 'You f*ing idiots. You have my f*ing anchor. Don't you f*ing damage my boat.'

I can't understand why he is so crazy mad, or why he took so long to tell us we were towing him.

'What would you like us to do?' Phil asks him politely.

Grumpy man is still busy yelling and swearing, but then he stops mid curse to say 'tie off the boats together.'

He drops his fenders and we tie our boat to his. It is not that easy with him cussing with every second word. 'F*ing idiot.'

I am sorry for Phil who is coming in for all the abuse, and normally I would jump in and apologise, but I have a feeling this time it would be better to keep my mouth shut.

For one thing, grumpy man is acting as if I am not even there. He yells at Phil and ignores me as if it couldn't possibly be my fault because I am only a female and obviously useless anyway.

The man is an idiot. A grumpy idiot.

I am sure he wouldn't appreciate an apology and besides, I am afraid that if I say anything I might burst into tears of frustration. I hate confrontation.

Phil hates confrontation too, but he is calm under pressure, and there is definitely pressure.

While the boats are tied together, both Phil and grumpy Man pull up their anchors and they come apart. We breathe a sigh of relief. Grumpy man pushes us away and offers a few more of the same phrases and then turns his back on us.

A man in a small blow-up boat has arrived and is trying to help. He seems bemused.

'Why did you keep moving forward?' he asks Phil as we push off from the other boat. I want to say 'because that idiot never told us there was a problem.'

Phil and I are quiet as we head over to Fitzroy Bay where we will stay the night. I was the one driving and Phil was directing me, so we both feel stupid for catching someone's anchor, but as Phil says, 'It is all learning and we won't do that again.'

'Grumpy Man will have a story to tell for years,' I say. 'It seems like an awful fuss about nothing. If he had been a reasonable man, he would have told us earlier that the anchors were too close and we could have had a good laugh together while fixing it.'

'I saw him following us,' I continue. 'He just stood there and glared. He could have said something.'

Phil is wonderful. He doesn't say anything.

This is exactly the sort of thing that attracted me to Phil when I first met him. He is calm under pressure. He doesn't waste time complaining, criticising, or blaming.

My first husband would have made it my fault. He would have started an argument, then sulked for the next week because I dared to disagree. There might even have been a physical fight with the owner of the other boat.

Phil focusses only on solving the problem and acts as if nothing is ever my fault, even when I could have done better.

In the new bay, we anchor our boat as far away from the other boats as we can manage.

Phil has been thinking. 'I wonder why he didn't say anything earlier.'

'I wonder that myself,' I say. 'He looked mad at us before we even moved.'

Phil thinks again. 'He must have known there was a problem with the anchor.'

More silence while he works it out in his mind. 'The more I pulled in my anchor, the more we drifted towards his boat. He must have laid his anchor across ours when he came in last night.'

And just like that, we both feel much better. It wasn't just our inexperience. Probably not even our fault.

There are still a few hours of daylight left, so we take Mini Manuka into the town, a tiny little village called Fitzroy Bay. We were warned it was just a shop and a pub but I can see neither.

I envisaged a big old-fashioned building with a veranda that looks out over the water, and a few friendly locals who don't see many visitors and want to know all about us. The reality is rather different.

Firstly, there are hardly any buildings here. Just a small dock with an attached shed, and a boat ramp, so we head for that.

As we near the boat ramp, we see five big men who seem to be having trouble getting into two small boats. They don't seem to be sure where they are going. One of the boats heads towards us, and then turns in a lazy circle until I wonder if they plan to play bumper boats. The men on board wave cheerfully but half-heartedly, as if they have just noticed us, and cannot remember who we are. They settle on a direction and head off. It looks as if the pub is (or was) open.

Behind the boat shed is a road. To the right it looks unsealed but it turns out to be covered in dirt from a landslide. To the left, the road leads to a nearby cluster of little buildings.

One of them has a sign outside that says 'Hot Food.' It is a removable sign and no one has removed it so we eagerly head over to the small shed-like building. A sign on the door says it is 'Fish and Chip Night on Friday' and we happen to have arrived on Friday. Both of us are very happy it is Friday.

Two people are standing in front of a window counter, and inside we can see a lady frying food. The fragrance of hot chips wafts out.

We wait behind the men as they talk to a lady standing by her car. None of these people seem to have noticed we are there. I wait for a chance to say hello but they act like city people in a packed train. The look past and around us as if we are invisible.

'What time does the shop close?' one of the men asks the cook.

A voice from inside calls out 'when I have finished the next order.'

Does that include us? I am not sure but since no one has acknowledged us, I feel unwelcome and wonder if the question is supposed to be a message to us.

I turn to confer with Phil and see him staring at the boat. He looks thoughtful then suddenly heads back to the boat, gesturing for me to follow. I realise he must have decided to give up.

'Yes,' I think. 'They don't deserve our custom or our money.'

But Phil has other things on his mind. 'I think the boat is drifting,' he says.

We run back to Mini Manuka and I fall into it in a hurry. Phil jumps in and starts the engine. He watches the boat carefully but doesn't seem to be heading back as fast as I expected.

'I don't think it is drifting after all,' he says. 'It is just a trick of perspective. It looks as if it has moved from the beach but only because of the way the land is shaped.'

Later, as we sit on the boat eating a warming chilli and rice dinner with mango rice pudding for dessert, I almost feel glad we missed out on fish and chips. We watch fog rolling in across the water, bringing a bank of heavy rain.

It is a nice night to go to bed early, and to read while raindrops patter on the deck above.

I love that I am in a beautiful part of the world sharing an adventure with the man I love. Today was stressful. Both Phil and I hate confrontation, but I think we handled it well. I smile to myself and then share my happy thought with Phil.

'I hope grumpy man is not married. I would hate to be his wife,' I say. 'I am so glad I am married to you.'

And the thought makes us both happy.

# Waterfalls and Walks in Fitzroy Bay

During the night I am woken several times by a noise that sounds as if the anchor is moving across a rocky ocean bottom. By the time the morning arrives, I am relieved to see we haven't hit any of the other boats. They seem to be as just as far away as they were when we went to bed.

We have another week before we need to back in Brisbane, and two weeks before Phil has to be back at work. We don't have to be anywhere in a hurry. I would like to explore some of the outer bays on Great Barrier Island but the weather report is for more bad weather with high winds and big seas, so we decide to stay here inside the island where it is more protected.

I make porridge for breakfast and finish watching the movie 'Singing in the Rain.' I watched half of it a few nights ago while Phil slept, and a little more last night before bed. I haven't been able to stay awake long enough at night to watch a whole movie all at once. Being here in a protected bay where the boat rocks gently like a porch swing all night, has been relaxing. I love these lazy evenings and slow mornings.

Late in the morning, when we finally feel motivated to do something, we take Mini Manuka in to explore the town some more. I am not sure what to expect. Everyone seemed unfriendly last night, as if they were a community created for one of Steven King's horror novels.

This time we park on the other side of the boat ramp where there is a small low jetty with other blow-up tenders attached to it. The first couple we meet, ask us to pass the water hose across to their tender. They seem very friendly so we ask them about the island. They direct us to a shop and information centre just over the rise in the road.

At the information Centre, I go in and talk to the attendant while Phil waits outside. It is smaller than the bedroom on our yacht and there is no room for three people. It is just a large cupboard filled with leaflets and other tourist information.

The attendant says there used to be picturesque wooden dams we could walk to, but they have been washed away in the same heavy rains that covered the road in dirt from the hillside. She suggests we walk to the local waterfall.

Before we go, we head up to the shop and wander around trying to decide what we need. We have our deodorant and chippies in hand before we realise it would be more sensible to get them after our walk instead of carting them around the island.

The owner is the same lady who was standing by the takeaway shop yesterday pretending we were not there. She looks unhappy with life in general and does not seem to particularly care if we buy anything, or just take it for a walk around the shop. We explain anyway.

'We will come back after our walk,' I say. She mumbles something, but neither of us can tell what.

We nickname her Sunshine Sally and spend the first part of our walk wondering if she is resentful because she is stuck here on the island while we all come and go. Perhaps her husband loves boats and she can't get him to leave. Perhaps he is grumpy man. I would probably look like her if I was married to him.

Before we take our one-hour trek into the bush, we get burgers from the same takeaway shop where we stood hoping for fish and chips. It is not as if there is any choice. There is nothing else around except a closed-up building advertising scuba diving lessons.

The cook takes my order and she seems very friendly, but it wasn't her that was so frosty yesterday. It was her customers.

We sit on a wobbly picnic bench while we wait. When my name is called, Phil gets up to get it and I nearly topple over. The bench is badly balanced.

When Phil comes back, he doesn't have our order. Another man at the opposite table seems to have it. I am confused until I realise the obvious. I catch his eye and innocently ask 'Is your name Nikki too?'

'No,' he says bluntly. 'I have been waiting for my order for an hour.' He dismisses us by putting his head down and is eating his burger (our burger?) as if he is taking part in an eating race. Neither Phil nor I can tell whether he has our order or the shop attendant called the wrong name.

A loud crash comes from behind one of the parked cars, and someone calls out for help. No one else moves but we decide to head over and see if we can do anything to help.

An elderly lady in a flower print house dress has fallen off the same sort of seat we are on and her chips are all over the ground. She seems to be okay and her family is there to pick her up and reassure her, so we go back to our own seat. We sit opposite each other to keep the wobbly seat balanced and when our burgers are ready, we decide it might be safer to eat them on the way to the waterfall.

I am not sure if it is the burger, or the steep walk up the road to the waterfall path, but stomach cramps come on rather suddenly and I am not sure what to do. I need a toilet urgently and I am fairly sure that the only public one is back at the village area on a hill just above the information centre.

I briefly consider whether there is enough cover at the side of the road before Phil makes the decision for me. We have to go back.

This is a small island with probably not much water, so the community facility here is situated over a deep hole in the ground. As I unroll the paper, a cloud of black insects rises into the air, but other than that, I am relieved to see the place is clean.

And now we have to walk up that steep hill for the second time, but it won't do me any harm. We don't get to do much walking on a boat like ours

This time we make it to the track and it is different from the forest areas in Australia where I do most of my walking now.

Brisbane is hot and wet in summer and warm and dry in winter. Many of the trees are grey or dry looking, often starved for water for months at a time. Here the trees are green and dense, lush with ferns and twisted vines.

We cross some wooden paths and bridges and, after about half an hour, we arrive at the waterfall and the peace is shattered by what seems like a child's voice coming from the hill above.

There is a man at the bottom of the cliff, and he doesn't seem concerned. I can see someone small at the top of the steep slippery rocks and it looks awfully dangerous. I wonder why the man is not insisting they come back down.

Then the man starts to climb up and I realise that he looks elderly. Fit and healthy, but older, maybe a grandfather. The other person starts to climb down and I see that I have been wrong there too. It is not a child that has been climbing the cliff and calling out, but an older woman, probably the man's wife.

I am amazed, and inspired by the couple's agility and spunk. They look older than us and so daring. I can't even climb an indoor rock wall with a safety harness and Phil at the other end. Here she is scrambling back down a precarious rock face as if she is an energetic and gutsy ten-year-old.

They comment on the damage done by a recent storm and as we walk back from the waterfall on another path, we see what they mean. There are large patches of fallen trees and damaged ground.

110

WATERFALLS AND WALKS IN FITZROY BAY

When we get back to the road, we meet a man collecting rocks from the road verges. He tells Phil he is collecting flat rocks to make a path in his garden. While we are walking down the steep road back to town, he overtakes us and we meet him doing the same thing further down.

'We just passed someone doing the same thing as you,' says Phil. Without missing a beat, the local says 'It's a common thing to do here. Soon there will be no rocks left.'

Before we go back to the yacht, we go pick up a few groceries from 'Sunshine Sally'. We get the deodorant we need and many things that we don't need; ice blocks, cool drinks, chicken chippies, and postcards to send to our boys. We do our best to elicit a smile from the shop assistant, but she is too tough for us.

The Information Centre is still open so I pop in to ask about the local hot pools.

'Do you have a car?' the lady asks. I shake my head.

'Well, you could hire one or walk to the end of the road and ask for a lift. Maybe someone will pick you up. Otherwise, it will take most of a day to get there and back.'

We are leaving tomorrow, so that nips that idea in its obviously laborious bud.

Back at the boat, I rest and read, Phil greases the engine, and the weather winds up for a big blow. It starts lightly, but builds up over the next few hours until there are odd gusts of wind that seem shot from a celestial cannon. Our boat swings this way and that, re-setting off my fears that our anchor is moving. I can even hear that same 'anchor over ocean rocks' sound I heard yesterday.

For several hours it alternately rains and gusts. I wonder how bad it is outside this sheltered bay, when it is this bad here, with hills on all sides. The open ocean must be wild.

In the early evening, we play a quirky card game with questions like 'What is Shoofly Pie?' and 'Who is the Bobby Pin named for?' until it gets too dark to read the words on the cards.

111

Phil starts the engine so we can have hot water for a shower and we go to bed soon after dark.

All we have to worry about now are the wind gusts that howl through the rigging like an icy Alaskan storm and then toss the boat around on her anchor as if we are sailing in circles. After the nights we had early on our trip, I expect this to be one of our more restful nights. Yet again, I am wrong.

# Leaving for the Bay of Islands

The night is a shocker. We are in bed at a reasonable time but I spend a long time just listening to the wind. It is gusty. Not just little bursts, but huge gale force thrusts that send our boat sideways and make everything on the masts rattle. In between it is just quiet enough to make each gust a shock.

Several times Phil gets out of bed to check we have not moved. He has installed a program on my phone to set off an alarm if we go any distance from where we anchored. Four times during the night it sets off a tinny and penetrating alarm. Each time Phil assures me that it is just that it can't read the GPS, or that it is reading wrong. 'We haven't moved,' he says.

Then he gets up to recharge it because this amazing and useless, poor excuse for a safety program has worn itself out, waking us up for nothing.

I am less than impressed. What use is an alarm that keeps us awake and doesn't tell us anything?

By mid-morning, the storm seems to have worn itself out, so I do a little washing, and then hang it on the rail to dry.

'We are ready to leave. Better move your washing,' Phil says.

'I just put it there,' I say

He patiently points out that the washing is just a foot and a bit above the water. As we leave the protection of the bay, it will likely get sprayed by sea foam. With our luck, it might even be under water in a few minutes. I bring it inside and we set off for the open ocean with wet clothes dripping from all the available indoor surfaces.

As we exit the last sheltered bay, a catamaran that is sailing ahead of us, turns around suddenly and heads straight back towards us. He is slightly to our right, but passes across our front so he can be on the correct side according to maritime rules. He seems to come unnecessarily close.

'I guess there are as many bad drivers on the ocean as there are on land,' I say.

When we reach the open sea, a new thought comes to mind. 'It was too rough for him,' I say. 'He was going out to sea but changed his mind.'

Our boats bounces as if there are potholes in the ocean but we have almost two weeks under our belts and have no intention of turning back. We laugh at how brave we have become.

The wind is roughing up the waves, turning the tops of some into white foam. I look across and wonder if someone could surf on one of these. Maybe if it was closer to town they would.

The boat is bobbing up and down and all but surfing down the tiny peaks, and my stomach begins to bounce around too.

'It's as if we are riding on the teacups ride at Disneyland crossed with the bumper boats again,' I say to Phil. 'I don't feel so good.'

I begin to yawn, which was what led into sea-sickness earlier. Rather than lose my breakfast, I go to bed. I sleep for a few hours, but wake up when a large spray of ocean makes it into my bedroom and splashes my side of the bedsheet. Luckily, I am sleeping on Phil's side.

The boat is enjoying its first favourable wind since we set off. It bounds along in great glee, while occasional waves bounce over the front of the boat and wash across our cabin roof and down our front windows. Once I get used to the fact that we are not sinking, I realise we are making great progress.

'She is going just over nine knots,' Phil says.

I am impressed. After days at less than a third of that, it is great news and might get us out of this stomach-churning ocean a little faster. I do a quick calculation. Nine knots is equal to about ten miles per hour. We were at walking speed. Now we are at jogging speed. Even an elephant can run faster than that. Perhaps not so impressive after all.

I begin to wonder if sailing might not be a rip-off. If it is good weather and a lovely sunny, calm day on the water, then there is no wind to sail. The only time you can get up any speed is when the wind churns the ocean until I am bouncing around like a lotto ball in its rotating drum.

I wedge myself into a corner of the cockpit again and then Phil needs me to move so he can adjust the sails. I climb up to the other end of the seat on the high side and brace my foot to stop myself falling back. Then he needs that side too.

I can't sit inside the cabin because the walls close in and I get sick. I wait for a wave, and slide back down to the low side until he needs it again. When do we get to the relaxed, do nothing sailing that he promised?

I spend some time trying to shut the doors into the back cabin after a second large splash sends spray into the bedroom again. Then I realise I need my jumper from the back cabin as the wind is getting chilly. It is too much trouble to open the doors again so I find something else to wear.

Every tricky manoeuvre, like opening a cabin door, will most certainly end in painful bumps and I risk sustaining more bruising or worse. I already have enough marks on my body for Phil to offer to connect the dots with a pen, so I prefer to do as little as possible.

It is another challenging day. When just opening a door is so difficult that I break into a sweat, there doesn't seem much point in trying to do anything other than hold on.

The good thing is that the wind keeps drying the sea water from the bedsheets, even though they are still on the bed. My bed will be dry tonight, but there will probably be salt on my pillow. It's a compromise.

Phil decides to make a hot drink for us both and I have never admired him more. Degree of difficulty? Probably eleven out of ten. I know I am not willing to try.

We boil water in a saucepan over a portable gas stove. It sits on the remains of the old oven, which is at least gimballed, i.e., it swings freely in a way that is supposed to keep it level when the boat is acting like a giant teeter-totter.

Last time I made hot drinks in high seas, I watched the water swing so high, I was sure it was going to tip all over the floor and flood over my feet. Today the rolling seems worse. When Phil appears with a hot chocolate drink for him and cup of hot soup for me, I am very impressed. And grateful.

I haven't been able to eat much. I still feel a little queasy, and the hot soup at least puts something warm in my stomach.

As night falls, I head off to bed, and leave Phil for a few hours. The autopilot is playing up again. Every few minutes, it locks up and Phil has to thump it to get it going again.

We decide to stop sooner rather than later and choose Whakamumu Bay. It looks quiet, protected from the wind, and there is an old whaling station there. We won't get there until 2am but at least we will get some sleep.

The Bay of Islands is only another ten nautical miles, but there is a cape to go around and yachts to avoid and we would prefer not to do either in the dark of the night.

At 1.30am I wake up and Phil is asleep in the front cabin. The sea is so calm, just little light reflecting mounds in the water, and the boat is barely moving. Phil wakes up and looks guilty.

He jumps up and goes outside to put down the sails because there is no wind and they are not doing anything. For once he does not harness himself in. In fact, he doesn't even put on his life jacket. I'm not sure if he has woken up properly.

At least the sea is now calm. It is less likely he will be tossed off into the sea.

For the next hour and a half, we motor at an excruciatingly slow speed along the coast and into the bay. As we reach our destination, I am surprised to see lights. There are other boats here, including a well-lit fishing boat. Phil goes to stand on the front deck of the boat while I steer. I have taken my contact lenses out for the night, so am effectively blind, but I have faith in Phil and this works really well. All I have to do is follow his instructions.

'A little left. Now right. Slow down. Reverse gently.' It works a treat and we end up anchored in the middle of the bay. We are well away from other boats, but they might be wishing we were even further away.

Putting down our anchor is a noisy process, as the chain clanks over metal ratchets, drowning even the noise of the engine, I wonder how many people we have woken up.

At 3am, we go to bed and the whole bay can finally get some sleep.

# Whale Hunters Bay

We wake up late to a picture postcard perfect bay. There are craggy green hills on three sides, and gently undulating water lapping the shores. As we get ourselves ready to explore the bay, all but one of the other boats leave.

'Don't they like us?' Phil asks, but I am glad to enjoy the quiet with just one other yacht.

I feel like a substantial breakfast, but we are out of eggs, and potatoes, and without a fridge, bacon is a distant memory. I make noodles. Then I make pineapple slices fried in pancake mix. It is not as bad as it sounds.

We move the rubbish bag to the rear hold, put away the washing hanging on every available line space and stray electrical wire, and try to make the place look tidy. Then we blow up Mini Manuka again and head to shore.

The whaling station is just a collection of old rusty tanks and machinery parts, with a few bricks and concrete pads thrown in for good measure. There is not much left of the buildings, but it is fascinating. There are signs with pictures of how it used to look and information about the whaling days. It is sad, as well as interesting.

They used to kill ten whales a year at this location, using spears thrown from boats not much bigger than Mini Manuka. Then they got a new bigger boat and started to kill fifty whales a year. It sounds terrible now when everyone is aware that whale populations have been decimated, but in the days before electricity and plastic, whales were an important resource. As well as providing meat for food, the oil was used in many things including lamps and soap.

Then there was baleen and ambergris.

Baleen is the substance whales have instead of teeth and is a kind of straining system, similar in composition to our fingernails. It was used in corsets, fishing poles, skirt hoops, umbrella ribs, carriage springs, and buggy whips. Personally, I am very happy without corsets, skirt hoops and buggy whips, but back then they were as important as our cell phones are today.

And then there is ambergris, an ugly greyish substance produced in the whale intestine and then either vomited out, or expelled at the other end. Improbably, it was highly prized by perfume makers.

Times were different then and they did what they thought they needed to do.

I imagine what it must have been like to see so many whales. I wonder if they felt as mixed about killing the whales, as Phil and I did about killing the fish I caught. It has to be done if you want to have fish to eat or whale meat for oil, but it is not fun. Did they get used to it? I guess so. Being a whaler was apparently an honourable profession.

I wonder if future generations will feel about our mining the earth, the way we feel about whaling.

As we motor back in Mini Manuka, we take the long way around the shore. This is the relaxing part of sailing, exploring in pretty bays.

I am not in a hurry to get back into that open ocean. Our next leg, is a journey around the cape to the Bay of Islands. The map says there is a current, but when we get closer, the problem for us is the lack of breeze, and we have to motor yet again. After doing up to eight knots the day before I am disappointed to feel like a snail again. Watching the cape get closer and then crawl past is like watching paint dry, or grass grow. I am bored so I check the map.

'It says this area is great for catching Kingfish,' I tell Phil. 'I should put out a fishing line.'

'You will need a stronger line,' he says. 'And bigger muscles.'

'There are also crayfish here,' I say hopefully. But Phil didn't bring any SCUBA gear and we never even considered bringing crayfish pots of our own.

I sit back resigned, but then we round the cape and there is a surprise.

A tourist boat alerts us to the presence of something worth seeing. We have found the 'Hole in the Wall.'

When my boys were young, I took some of them on a camping trip and the boat trip we took to the 'Hole in the Wall' was a highlight. I had looked for this spot on the map and couldn't work out where it was. Now we have found it by accident.

The tourist boat stops on one side of a large arched opening in the rock and everyone on board seems to be up on deck and looking out.

We motor over, avoiding other yachts that are doing the same, and watch as the boat waits for just the right wave pattern and then powers through the narrow passage. A second boat follows the first and even from a few hundred yards away, I can hear the people on the second boat, screaming with excitement.

I am excited too. I loved this place. If only we didn't have a tall mast, we could go through too. Although we might need a stronger motor. And a braver crew. It is a narrow gap and the water is white and foamy, hinting at submerged rocks. It's probably best left to the experts.

Because we have rounded the cape, we are not heading into the wind anymore, so Phil puts up the sails. Then he puts down the sails. There is still not enough wind. We are still motoring. It has surprised me how much motoring we have needed to do.

Phil assures me again that when we are full time boaties, there will be no hurry. We will motor less when we have time to follow the wind.

While it is calm, I decide to be daring and make burritos for our late lunch. It is a tricky process, involving a burrito kit, a can of beans, a can of tomatoes and three little cans of cooked chicken. I sticky up so many plates and bowls that washing up is a complicated and messy process, but they are a success. Phil likes them and I am happy enough with the result. They are not bad considering we have no fresh food aboard.

Now we are around the last cape, we are in the Bay of Islands. There are bays galore and each more beautiful than the last.

The islands and rock formations are all shapes and sizes from skinny pointed teeth, to low rounded mounds. One island is narrow in the middle, as if some giant hand has nipped it between thumb and finger and pressed it into a slim neck of sand. There are sleeping dragons, and hippos, and alligators, and one with a Mohawk haircut of trees.

It seems to take another age as we crawl closer to Russell where we plan to stop. I am getting tired of taking so long to get anywhere. Every other boat on the water goes faster than us. Huge freighters pass us from behind, even when they start out on the horizon.

Little yachts cruise past, and the small motor boats run rings around us. The only good thing is that we go so slow that we are unlikely to run into anything. If by any chance we did hit something, it would have to be the other boat's fault. They have plenty of time to change course and avoid us.

When I was a teenager, I challenged a friend to a slow pushbike race. The winner was the one who could take the longest to get to the end without falling off the bike or leaving the path. I was good at that. I am not good at this. I like visiting new places and can't wait to get there.

This is a bit like watching snails in a race, only with more depth and less action. It is like an illusion. Nothing seems to change and we don't seem to get any nearer. I have to look away for a long while or have a two-hour nap before I notice any change in the scenery

I decide to steer as at least it will help the time pass. It is hard to keep the boat on track with the waves bouncing it around from side to side. I dare not look away. When I do, the waves jerk the boat onto a new course. My arms get tired of constantly readjusting the wheel.

Other boats race past and I am jealous. If I could walk on water, I might be tempted to get out and go and see what is ahead. I am sure I could walk faster than this.

It is a relief when we finally round that last point and see the town of Russel before us. We anchor as far from the other boats as we get without losing the shelter of the nearby hills.

Even though it is still daylight when we arrive, we decide not to go into town. We are both worn out from the strenuous work of the last few hours. As it turns out, Russell is well worth the trouble we have taken to get here.

# Russell. Sin City.

In the morning, I get up so early, I beat the sun out of bed. For the first time I notice that daylight seems to come much later here than in Brisbane.

Since I am up, I decide to do some writing, but it doesn't last long. I head back to bed for a quick snooze, and Phil and I both fall asleep again. Another late start. We have porridge for breakfast and then head off to town in Mini Manuka.

Russell is the most beautiful town. The waterfront is lined with buildings with second story verandas and old-fashioned store fronts. There are pohutukawa trees along the beach fringe and café seats overlooking the water. It is so pretty; I take hundreds more photos.

We start our visit at Pompellier House, an old Catholic Church building that used to be a print shop. We are in time for a tour, but it is mostly made up of teenagers from a local school so it is difficult to get to the front for a good view. Even so, I learn a lot, including the origins of the phrases, 'skiving off' and 'to coin a phrase'.

We are told that Catholic priests in Russell wrote books by hand until a French bishop bought this property and set up the print equipment. Paper was brought from overseas, and the pages were typeset, letter by metal letter and set into phrases with a 'Quoin' around them to confine them securely for printing. The guide tells us that this is where 'To coin a phrase comes from.'

Downstairs, under the veranda, they show us where they prepared the leather to cover the books.

Hides were first soaked in urine collected from chamber pots in the town. After a week, the leather was removed and soaked in tanning fluid for a complete year. Each day, it was taken out and dried so that more fluid would soak into the cloth when it was dropped back in.

Hands up to not do that job.

When it was ready, a skiver would strip off the hair with a sharp blade and then others would pound it with wooden strikers with curved bottoms and grab handles. The skiver was believed to have the easiest job, so anyone who takes it easy, is charged with 'skiving off.'

It was a complicated and back-breaking process and I am surprised to hear that when it was operational, they printed and bound forty thousand bibles in the Māori language and then gave them away for free.

As we walk out through the inevitable gift shop, I am tempted to buy one of the lovely old notebooks they have for sale. They are made by hand using the same complicated and traditional process (presumably including the urine soaking) but they cost too much for me.

After a visit to the small museum, we have no problem spending twice the cost of a book, on a delicious seafood chowder, an all-day breakfast for Phil, some curly fries and two iced chocolates. With all that in our stomachs we decided to walk for a bit. Time to find a geocache.

Our first find is two streets from the beach and is rather exceptional.

There is a bench seat here with a frame over it and two life-sized toy animals perched jauntily on the chair. Hanging from the frame are two metal sieves attached to wires. If you sit in the right spot, you can put the sieves on your head and look as if you are having electric shock treatment. There are old power station cast-offs to add to the illusion and a sign saying 'Caution, Live Wires.' The cache is cleverly concealed inside a hollowed-out bolt.

Even better the seat has an interesting story. The home behind it, used to belong to a school teacher. She lived to be 97 years old and each year, the school children would come and sing to her. The seat was built in her memory and the house is now owned by a family member.

Of all the geocaches I have ever found; this has to be a favourite.

I enjoy it so much, that I persuade Phil to walk up and over the nearby hill to find two more caches at seats. Neither is as creative as the first one, but they both have beautiful views over the ocean and the town. I can't help thinking it would be a stunning place to live.

Our last stop is at Christ Church, the oldest church in New Zealand. It is a postcard pretty, inside as well as out. Every seat had a cross stitched cushion with a variety of themes from sailing ships, to wildlife, to local scenes.

Outside, the grounds are full of interesting graves and headstones of men who drowned with their ships, and babies who died of disease. One tiny grave has a poem.

*The sweetest bud that never grew, and God*
*has taken her home to blossom above.*

I am reminded of a time when my own six children were babies and how exceedingly grateful I am that they are all still well and healthy.

After a quick trip to stock up on drinks and chocolate, we escape with our booty back to the yacht and have a short rest.

I call my dad. He is relieved to hear from me and I realise he thinks we might be bang in the middle of the Tasman Sea, right amongst the cyclones. I have been posting updates to Facebook, but he is not on Facebook and hasn't seen them.

He lives in a retirement village where everyone is old and most of the residents are women. He has me laughing as he talks about the predictability of each day.

'At morning tea time.' he says, 'some lovely old dear always asks me what I have planned for the day. It's a retirement village, so what can I say? I told one lady I was planning to do a high dive into a circus bucket and then take a turn on the high wire. She wasn't amused. No one has a sense of humour here.'

I sympathise but at least he is happier than my mum. She is in a secure residential home suffering from dementia and talking to herself in the mirror.

When I am off the phone, Phil suggests we go exploring in Mini Manuka. I jump at the chance and naturally I choose this opportunity to look for a geocache.

As we arrive at the bay, it is deserted, but when we get out of the boat, two girls walk out of the bush. I assume they are here for the geocache, it is too much of a coincidence, but I am wrong. They are here to take sunset photos of the bay. It is a lovely sunset and I might have taken one or two dozen photos myself during our search.

The cache is under a tree near a boggy piece of ground that sucks my feet in and slurps them out. I have mud up to my ankles when we walk over and meet the girls. They are from Sri Lanka but live in Perth and Melbourne. No surprise to meet some Aussies here.

As we motor back in Mini Manuka, the setting sun casts a golden glow around, and the twilight makes the bay a different kind of beautiful. The other yachts are tinged with a soft glow, and the water sparkles as lights turn on in the town across the bay.

Even though it is now dark, we decide to carry on into town for fish and chips. As we head for the shore, I am splashed by a wave generated by a passing boat and water splashes down my back.

It must look as if I have wet myself. It is not a good way to arrive in town, but it is dark and I hope no one will notice. Plus, we will get take-away, then it won't matter.

We wander around for a bit and can't find a suitable take-away shop. We end up back at the same place we had lunch. A restaurant called Sally's. I apologise for being rather damp.

'We serve a lot of yacht owners,' she says as if people walk in here with wet pants all the time, and then she ushers us to a surprisingly public spot.

We forgo the fish and chips and splash out on lamb shoulder, and more fish chowder. It is the same chowder I had for lunch and it is superb. It even comes with the name of the restaurant written on the chowder with cream.

From where we sit, we look out over the many boats anchored in the bay and the lights of Pahia on the other side. It could not have been more magic, even if I did leave the seat a little wet.

Our night ends with a moonlit ride in Mini Manuka, dodging boats in the dark, and admiring the clear view of the stars. I can't think of a better way to get home.

# Historic Waitangi

There are two kinds of nights on this trip. There are the really awful nights when we are at sea, and the boat shifts and tosses. The nights where I have to sleep with my arms open wide to stop myself falling out of bed. The nights with a tractor engine right next to my head or the constant flapping, roiling of the sails and the thudding of water against hull, or both. Nights when someone has to be alert for ships on the horizon and sleep is a luxury for me and an impossibility for Phil.

Then there are the quiet nights at anchor. I like the quiet nights best, but even these are not usually peaceful. Now that I am over fifty, I sometimes need to get up at night.

A trip to the forward cabin in the dark can be eventful, even when the boat is not moving. Up the bedroom ladder, across the cockpit area, down the steps into the main area, turn on a light, step over the foot-high door step, and into the too small bathroom where I have to squeeze myself into the toilet space.

Back to the main cabin to turn on the water pump which I always forget, and then back to the bathroom to wash my hands.

Then I do it all in reverse to get back to bed, remembering to straddle the tiny bedroom floor, one foot on the lowest step and another below the cupboard so I don't make the floor squeak and wake Phil. It is an adventure I could do without.

Last night I was up twice, and both times I stopped to check the GPS to make sure we had not drifted on our anchor.

Phil did not set the anchor app, but I marked the spot on our GPS where we started the night. Our spot has moved. I am awake for an hour at 3am, checking periodically because I am sure we must be drifting out to sea.

In the morning, I tell Phil we have moved.

'Yes,' he says. 'I let out the anchor last night before bed.'

I lost sleep for nothing.

Because we have done a lot of motoring and want to keep the fuel topped up, we sail over to the Russell wharf to fill up the diesel tank again. As we approach, there is a ferry berthed here and two sailors on board are watching us closely. We are both nervous as this could go badly. I pick up the forward rope and stand at the front ready to lasso one of the large poles and pull us in.

That part goes surprisingly well. Now we are secure at the front, Phil puts the engine in reverse and turns the rudder hard to one side, but instead of moving the back sideways into the dock, the current stops the back from moving. Then, the front of the boat bangs against the dock and shudders the whole structure, including the one where the ferry is docked. Our back end stays stubbornly out to sea. I don't dare look at the two sailors.

I offer to climb across the front and attach a rope further back, then when I attempt to do so, I realise I am too chicken to jump across the gap from boat to wharf. It is much higher and wider than I am comfortable with.

Phil makes the climb easily, and I hand him a rope. He pulls on the rope and I reverse the engine and after some time, she floats in at her usual leisurely pace. Tourists on the beach take photos and then wander off, and then a new ferry arrives. A large group of passengers wander down the dock and watch us with interest.

It is a strange thing to be part of the attraction in this town we barely know.

When we have finished entertaining the visitors with our antics, we cross the bay to Waitangi.

This area is sometimes referred to as the birthplace of New Zealand. It was here that the Treaty of Waitangi was written and signed in 1840, making New Zealand a British Colony and the Māori people subjects of the British Queen.

It is a large tract of grassy land overlooking the bay and although I have been here before, it was at night and I didn't see much. I am looking forward to seeing it again.

We find a suitable anchoring spot and motor to the beach in Mini Manuka. An official in a blue shirt with the Waitangi logo wanders down to meet us and informs us that we cannot arrive by sea.

'I have never heard of a Māori custom that stops people arriving by boat to an event,' I say to Phil as we head back to the yacht. 'Perhaps it is sacred ground where the land meets the shore.'

I have lived most of my life in New Zealand and feel disappointed that I can't educate Phil in the ways of the Māori in the same way that he has taught me Aussie slang.

We head over to the local boat club to see if we can fill up our water tanks. The yacht club asks for $10 'donation' for water, so I make the most of it and do a few loads of hand washing while the tanks fill.

Washing our clothes is tricky in the confined space of the on-board bathroom but I would rather do it this way than spend another day sitting on plastic chairs in a dingy laundromat, watching my washing go around and around for two hours.

When we are done, we pack up and push away from the wharf. The front goes out and the back goes in and there is a big bang and we have broken off the only remaining piece of our davit. It leans drunkenly to one side, sheared off where it used to meet the deck.

The side that fell off on one of our earlier trips, is already tied to the railing. Phil ties this new piece next to the first piece using a length of green striped rope. They sit together looking like two dirty old bits of pipe (mostly because they are dirty old bits of pipe).

We have no davit at all now, just broken metal ends where it used to be, but I am not sure if anyone will notice. There is so much wrong with this ship, another broken bit is not really noticeable, even if it does stick out at a crazy angle and serve no purpose.

There have been two ladies fishing on the wharf next to us the whole time and I try to avoid their eyes. They seem to be glaring as if we are disturbing them, and I am tempted to glare back. We were told to stop here and we have enough problems without the added risk of snagging a finishing line and dragging one of them into the ocean with our propeller.

We take the yacht back out to the open water and park across from the Waitangi grounds. I hang some of our wet washing outside to dry, folding it carefully, to make it look less like washing and more like flags. Then we take Mini Manuka back to the boat club and leave it tied up at the wharf while we walk to the front entrance of the Waitangi grounds. I am still curious about the reason we couldn't land on the beach.

A short walk later and we are parting with $50 for entry to Waitangi and the mystery is solved. It is not because of any Māori custom that we can't land on the beach. Simply a more modern desire to make a profit.

At least the entrance fee is worth paying. Someone has put a lot of time and effort into the displays and I relearn a lot of things I was taught as a young school child but have simply forgotten.

The Treaty of Waitangi is a written agreement that the British have sovereignty over New Zealand, both colonists and Maori.

It has united, divided, and confused people ever since. Maybe because it was put together over the course of just a few days.

William Hobson arrived in the Bay of Islands on the 29th January 1840 with the intention of governing a colony which had not yet been formally created. He and his secretary wrote the original notes, James Busby, a British Official, compiled the notes into a document, and Henry Williams, a missionary, translated it into Māori. Both versions were presented to around five hundred Māori at a meeting at Waitangi, on the 5th of February 1840.

All day and into the night the visitors and officials debated the treaty, then the next day, forty chiefs agreed to sign it.

Over the next nine months, at least nine copies of this treaty were made and taken around the country and signed by more than five hundred Māori chiefs, including five women. Most of the chiefs signed a Māori language version, and thirty-nine signed an English version.

It has been the subject of many court cases, and since 1974, millions of dollars have been paid to various indigenous groups who have sought compensation for breaches of the guarantees set out in the treaty.

The house at Waitangi is surprisingly small for an official government residence. When James Busby first lived here with his soon to be six children, it was an even smaller two bedroomed house. He wrote to his superiors to complain. He said 'How am I supposed to be taken seriously by the natives when I don't even have a spare room to meet them in?'

That was only one of his problems. He had no powers and no military support but he had an impressive list of duties. He was:

*To check outrages by Europeans against the Māori, to protect 'well-disposed' British settlers and traders, and to seize escaped convicts. He was also to assist the Māori, if*

> *possible, to establish 'a settled form of*
> *government'.* [1]

He was also advised to:

> *Rely on the influence that an 'educated*
> *man possesses over the wild or half-civilized*
> *savage' and on the assistance of the*
> *missionaries and of visiting warships.*

Māori's today must be pleased to hear that.

His house might have been tiny, but his garden was huge and his outlook was glorious; right across the bay to the islands. I can only imagine how it would have looked with three separate gardens, flowers all around, a tree orchard, and a whole section of grape vines. James Busby was apparently well-known for his grapes.

Phil and I spend hours at the display, and then visit the two longboats (waka) that we had seen earlier from the yacht. The longest is made from one tree trunk and needs 79 people to row it. The tour guides are very proud to tell us that Queen Elizabeth once went for a ride in it and commandeered it as part of the British fleet.

When we arrived, we bought tickets to a concert inside the meetinghouse. It is about to start and as we approach, a very loud and entertaining Māori lady greets us and explains that we are going to follow protocol and will be greeted by warriors as we approach the building.

When she asks for a volunteer, I try to get Phil to put his hand up. He is a very private person and not interested but the lady has seen my efforts. She picks him to be our chief for the day.

Phil glares at me, but I am so proud, and even prouder, when the very warlike looking actors come out. The biggest and loudest of them approaches Phil, chanting in Māori and waving

---

[1] http://adb.anu.edu.au/biography/busby-james-1858

his spear, and then shoves it into Phil's face, missing his nose by a whisker. Phil doesn't even flinch.

Inside the meetinghouse, Phil has to give a speech on behalf of the small group of tourists watching the show today. He calls us his 'Motley Crew' and thanks them for what they are about to show us.

As chief, he and I have front row seats while the warriors continue to threaten with spears and Māori clubs. Unlike Phil, when they come my way, I flinch and dodge.

There are only seven performers including three ladies, but they are so energetic and loud that they fill up the hall and seem like many more. They sing and dance and then the whole group plays stick games (rakau) and swing balls on the end of ropes (poi).

I am surprised to find that while I watch the sticks flying and the balls swinging, my eyes are tearing up. I feel an emotional connection to the culture and it is something I have never felt before.

My adopted brothers are part Māori and my first husband, and all my sons are part Samoan. I have always been the English one, the one who didn't have a culture, at least not in the singing, dancing, and performing half-naked sense.

I suspect the performance has taken me back to a time when I was five years old and we used to play stick games and sing Māori songs at school. Perhaps it has also affected me because most of the others here are tourists, including Phil, but this is my 'home', and part of my culture as a kiwi.

After the show, as we walk through the bush back to Mini Manuka, I am reminded how much fun it is to get in a small boat at the end of the day instead of a car. There is always the risk of getting a bit wet, but it usually dries quickly, unless of course I am going out for dinner. At those times it seems I can stay embarrassingly damp for hours.

Back at the boat, the washing I have hung over the side of the boat is nearly dry, but the rest of it is still hanging damply all around the main cabin. I move some of our underwear up into the cockpit to get more wind, and we set off for Motuarohia Island, also known as Robertson's Island. It is just around the corner, but naturally it takes us hours to get there.

It is a tiny island, less than a mile at its longest point but famous because Captain Cook anchored here in 1769. At that time there was a Māori settlement with up to three hundred people living in a pa at the Eastern end of the island, but now it is almost deserted. Just a few houses and maybe one or two that have residents.

As soon as we arrive in the bay, I suggest we visit the island and walk across the narrow neck of sand in the middle. It's not far from getting dark, but Phil agrees to take me.

The internet insists that the two lagoons here are 'the most photographed spots in the Bay of Islands' but I am not impressed. It is low tide and all I can see are wet rocks in two great depressions. At least it means we can walk through to the other side.

The ocean on the far side is much more exposed with churning water and jagged rocks. It is very picturesque and dramatic but we don't stay long. It looks as if the tide is on its way in and we don't want to get cut off.

Back at the boat, we have a decision to make.

We will have to leave the yacht somewhere for a year, but it is not simple. Where should we be? Up north, close to where we will leave from when we do sail for Australia? In Auckland where it is closer to the airport and flights to Brisbane?

Maybe we should try to find someone to deliver it to Brisbane without costing us an arm, a leg, and several other limbs.

Even if we find someone, will they be able to cope with the engine that needs constant attention or the dodgy electrics? Will they be able to manage the temperamental autopilot, or survive the swinging cooker?

We have called people and emailed, and sent texts. We have studied websites and booklets. There is a lot to think about but we finally come to a decision. We choose a marina in Auckland.

We will still have to pay twice the rate we paid in Napier, but some of the other options cost even more, and at least we will be able to get to the airport easily.

I write in my diary, then make Thai Green Curry, courtesy of that awesome Hawkes Bay company that makes so many of the instant meals that I brought with us. Phil is quiet and I am not sure what to say. He has been dreaming of getting the yacht home for years but I am relieved.

With all that went wrong in our trip, ripped sails, damaged electrics, unresponsive autopilots, and engine failures, it would have been very scary to head to the middle of the ocean where there are no spare parts, no sailmakers, no electronic stores, and no chance of stopping for the night to get some sleep.

Subdued, we look at options for the next few days. We still have another week of holiday, but we need to head back down south so we will be back in port before the cyclone arrives.

The few days we spent on Great Barrier Island during bad weather were bad enough. Even though we were protected from the open ocean, the sea was gusty and rough, and the boat was given a good thrashing. We don't want to be exposed during another storm and this one is purported to be two cyclones joined together. It is bound to be worse.

We make short work of half a box of liquorice and then head for bed.

# Robertson's Island Streakers

It's not easy being stuck in a confined space with someone who keeps bursting out into the same song. Ever since I watched the movie 'Singing in the Rain', both of us keep singing but I am by far the worst. Phil is a saint to put up with me.

And it isn't even raining.

It's just another sunny summer day and we are about to go exploring the tiny island of Motuarohia. There are only a few houses on this island and we can see one from our boat. During breakfast, we watch an older couple leave the house and walk along the beach. I assume that means there is somewhere worth walking. There is supposed to be a Māori Pa here but we haven't seen any signs. Perhaps we can ask this couple.

We set off for the shore in our little blow-up boat and start along the beach towards the couple. As we get closer, one of the people is walking to the water. I look over at Phil.

'It looks as if one of them is swimming naked,' I say.

Neither of us has great eyesight for distance, so we can't really tell. This is the only path here anyway so we keep on walking toward them. Then the second person takes off their robe, and Phil and I realise we were right.

They don't seem to have any clothes on and we are following them. That doesn't seem like such a good idea any more. As soon as we can, we move inland and take an uphill path.

141

I briefly wonder if that will ever be us. Swimming 'au natural' seems like such a brave thing to do, especially as you get older and less attractive.

The steep path we are on heads up into the bush and I am grateful that someone has gone to all the trouble of making it for people like us. When we reach the top breathing deeply, we find a wooden lookout with fabulous views in every direction.

We can clearly see the low spot that divides the island almost into two. On the side we are anchored, it is mild and there is a pebble beach. On the far side, there are steep bluffs, sharp rocks, and a dangerous looking foaming pool where the water comes in.

When we get back to the bottom, we see a sign that says there is a snorkelling trail in one of the pools. The naked couple has gone, so I wade in to the pool to look for it.

The water is very refreshing, and I tease Phil who waits patiently, but can't be persuaded into the water. His mid-winter swim in Antarctica was cold enough to ice up his eyelashes, but after a few years living in sunny Brisbane, he finds the New Zealand summer too cool to swim. Of course, I tease him.

The water in the pool is crystal clear. I can easily see where buff coloured sand becomes rocks of various earthy colours including rust. I wade in the water up to my waist, but the pool never gets deep and I can't find a snorkelling trail.

Back at the yacht, we have an early lunch, while several boats visit our little bay. A large new looking charter catamaran calls in long enough for Phil to wave at a family on board but doesn't stay.

A tourist boat comes through and passes really close to us as if we are in the very spot they want for themselves. I can hear the commentary but not make out all the words. I expect the tourists on the boat are hearing about the tragedy on this island.

In 1839, there was not just one, but a whole heap of murders here.

Maketu, a sixteen-year-old Māori boy working on the island, killed his supervisor because he felt he had treated him badly. The owner of the land was a widow named Mrs Robertson, and when Maketu told her what he had done, she was not sympathetic. She said he would be hanged. His response was to kill her as well, along with all her children. Then he set the house on fire.

Mrs Robertson was right. He was hanged - the first Māori to be tried and hung in New Zealand under colonial law.

I am sure the people on the tour boat should be fascinated by this story, but some of them are facing away from the island and taking photos of our boat.

'I wonder what they think of us,' I say to Phil. Phil suggests the captain is telling them that this bay is where old boats go to die.

I look around and think this is possible. Maybe even probable. We are looking particularly shabby. Both the davits are now just jagged ended rusty pipes tied on to the rails.

On each side of the mast there are ladders made from old mismatched pieces of wood, tied together with string. I ask Phil what he thinks. 'I guess the previous owner made them out of whatever he had on hand,' he says.

'But there is a missing step on one side,' I point out.

'Must have fallen off,' says Phil.

I look around. 'And why the stringy mop heads on the sides of the cross piece? Why is there garden hose covering one of the ropes?'

Phil says the mop heads protect the sail from the spreaders on the mast but he has no idea why there is green garden hose on two ropes that don't even seem to have a purpose.

When Phil is tired of me making fun of our boat, it is time to pull up the anchor and set off for Poor Knights Island. As is usual, pulling up the anchor is easier said than done.

I am in place all ready to steer wherever Phil needs me to, when Phil stops winching and comes inside.

'Can you believe it? The winch is broken.'

I can believe it.

Phil has to lift up the anchor and fifty feet of heavy chain, all by hand. I can tell it is arduous work because it takes nearly ten minutes and he has to take a break several times.

We motor for some time after that, probably because he is too tired to put up sails and I don't know how to help.

'The wind has picked up,' I say after an hour of laboured and noisy motoring.

Phil is good at taking a hint and he puts up the sails and turns off the engine. After ten minutes of infrequent wind gusts, sail adjustments, and slow progress, Phil pulls them in again and we motor once more. I can't seem to get away from that tractor noise.

It is worse for Phil. The way the engine is set up, he has to go into the bilge to turn the water tap on or off, each time he uses the engine. It may not be strictly necessary, but then again it may be. If the water leaks, we might end up with a bilge we could go swimming in. Phil feels it is worth the extra effort to ensure we stay afloat.

Phil then goes into the main cabin to look for something and the knob breaks off a cupboard. For a few hours, we have to open it with a screwdriver, then Phil knots a piece of string around it. It opens easily but it is not pretty. Then again, not much is pretty on this boat, at least not yet.

While he is still searching for something, he comes across the new boat shoes I bought for the trip. I could have used those this morning in the rock pools. These shoes are grey and white and look like dancing spats only made of rubber mesh. They are partly stylish, and yet also weird. I can't decide if I like them. Better late than never, I wear them for the next few hours, but they are tricky to take on and off and when they are off, they stay off.

A few hours out, the engine is still on, but Phil puts up the sails and we use both. Then he goes to bed for a nap.

The autopilot is not playing again. Every few minutes, the steering wheel stops moving and I have to knock it into action. If I don't notice, the boat drifts away in lazy circles towards the shore. It is tiring just staring at the steering wheel and waiting for it to stop juddering and freeze up. In the end I decide it is easier to steer myself.

Is everything on this boat going wrong?

The winch is not working. The autopilot has stopped working. The engine needs constant servicing, and there is not enough wind to sail. I am tired of the cacophonous engine noise, and it has given me such a headache.

I take some pain reliever. It sort of works.

There is one good thing about a rough crossing. There are hardly any other boats to watch out for. We have the ocean to ourselves today. Probably because no one else wants it.

When Phil wakes, I make milo, and soup, and we eat it with chicken chippies. I consider how much this is becoming like a road trip, only with less places to stop for junk food. The other day we had breakfast at 8am and lunch at 10.30am. Sometimes I eat just to pass the time, and there is plenty of time. If our car went this slowly, the roadside rescue team would offer to tow us home.

Another pod of dolphins joins us. Even though the deck is bouncing around as badly as ever, I go outside and wrap myself around a solid piece of boat so I can watch the dolphins play and cavort around us. I love dolphins and it helps pass another fifteen minutes.

It is a long afternoon and evening. We are heading for Poor Knights Island, a marine reserve with great reviews from people who have visited. The ocean is supposed to be teeming with fish, and the land bulging with interesting birds and wildlife. I am looking forward to it, but staring at the island is frustrating as it never seems to get closer. When it gets too dark to see anything, I go to bed.

In the middle of a peaceful dream, Phil wakes me. It is after midnight, and we have reached Poor Knights Island. He needs help to anchor, especially as the moon is hidden by clouds. It is pitch black and neither of us can see anything except one light that could be a warning light, a house on shore, or another boat. We decide to keep well away from it.

We watch our navigation program carefully because it is all we have to guide us. The moon is still hidden and there is nothing but blackness all around. The depth sounder is counting down the depth as we approach shore. Seventy-five feet, seventy-four feet. Slow but steady. Phil goes inside to check the navigation program again. It clearly shows our location, but has a delay of two seconds.

I am steering into a black void of nothingness until suddenly I am not. A huge shape appears reflected in the light from our mast. It looks substantial, but can only be clouds. I ask Phil.

'Is that clouds?'

Phil rushes up on deck and clarifies the obvious. It is a cliff face and we are heading right for it. 'Turn, turn,' he shouts.

'I can't,' I say. I am going so slowly that there is not enough speed to propel the boat in the desired direction. The steering wheel is unresponsive.

'Full power,' yells Phil.

So, in the face of a very tall and solid cliff face, I have to increase speed towards it before I can turn away. It is terrifying because neither of us can tell how far away the cliff is. I watch the tiny GPS map on my little phone because I cannot see our main program. The little arrow on the screen that is our boat, touches and passes right over the black line that defines the edge of the land.

As we complete the turn, my breath gradually returns to my body. Phil has another look at the map to see where we might anchor. It all looks the same. It is deep all the way to land, and now we know it is not a soft sandy beach, but a solid, unyielding cliff face, we are both tense and jumpy. My voice gets higher and faster and more demanding. It seems safer not to speak because I so want to shout at someone and it is not Phil's fault.

We try another spot, but the water never gets shallower than seventy feet and we are quite close to land. We might not have enough chain to anchor that deep, and even if we did, the winch is broken and Phil would need to pull it up by hand.

Phil decides that sailing through the night to the next island is safer than stopping here where the cliffs come out to meet us. As we start to head out, I am disappointed. I was looking forward to sleeping in a sheltered bay, and checking if the snorkelling here is as good as they say.

Visitors have described the marine life on this island as abundant and colourful and the seabed as filled with arches and caves. They leave comments on travel websites such as, 'Best diving in the world,' 'Worth crossing the world for,' and 'If I could dive only one place in the world, this would be it.'

I am grumpy that I will miss all this, but also relieved. I know I am lucky to be still sailing and not butted up against a cliff in a battered yacht.

Then the GPS plays up.

Phil watches the computer map carefully as I turn the boat to leave. 'Keep turning,' he says.

But the light that could be a yacht or a lighthouse, has gone full circle and is back on our right again. We are heading back to shore. It is two seconds more before the GPS catches up. By that time, we have made the decision to trust the light and are happily on our way out.

I go back to sleep and Phil sets our course for Hen and Chickens Island. It doesn't have as many Internet fans as Poor

Knights Island but it is also a marine reserve and has lots of birds. It will be a nice consolation prize.

Phil sets the radar alarm for every thirty minutes and joins me in bed. And then gets up to check. And then comes back to bed. And then gets up. All night long. Beep, beep.

About 4am, Phil asks if I really want to stop at Hen and Chickens Island. It would mean trying to anchor in the dark again.

'Plus,' he says 'the weather report says that in two days' time there is going to be cyclone. Not just the regular cyclone that we are expecting, but two cyclones that threaten to join together and become a super cyclone. Do you want to stop?'

'Not really,' I mumble. 'Perhaps it would be better if we kept going.'

Phil continues bobbing up and down for the rest of the night, and I toss and turn and try to sleep.

# Heading to Waiheke

Early in the morning, we lose a fan belt and Phil has to go down into the engine and change it. He wakes me up to steer again.

The sails are up, but the wind is desperately trying to push us into a nearby island. After the third time I have to force the steering wheel back to the left, I ask if we could go around the other side. Phil agrees. Anything to keep us moving. It is the long way around, but it is a good idea. It gives Phil enough time to change the fan belt and I stop feeling as if my arms are going to be pulled from their sockets.

I took my contact lenses out after the cliff face incident and even though it is daylight, everything is a touch blurry. Luckily, the island is big enough for even me to see.

It's just that nothing seems to change. We seem to be heading around the island for hours. I wonder if I have gone all the way around and then I spot a small rocky outcrop just past the island. It becomes a point of reference and stops me feeling as if I am stuck in a time warp.

When Phil takes over again, I turn on the gas stove to heat water for milo. It's scary standing by a swinging pan of boiling water, so I wait upstairs.

After a while, I notice a burning smell and Phil goes into the main cabin to check. He finds my contact lenses case blackened and melted in the flames. Luckily my lenses are now in my eyes, and not in the case. I stare sadly at the remains of the case as we drink our milo and eat pancakes.

After breakfast, Phil sets up the radar and the autopilot, which seems to be behaving today, and we both head back to bed for a cuddle and some much-needed sleep. Within minutes we are rudely awakened by the radars shrill beep. There is a boat on the horizon, but it is moving away.

I start to wonder if having a yacht like ours, is like having a toddler. Constant demands, interrupted nights, and never a quiet moment. 'Mum, the wind has changed. Dad, can you change my sails? My engine is hot. I need a new fan belt. That boat is looking at me.'

But like a toddler, it is all worth it. It is difficult and troublesome, but it is an adventure. You don't get adventure without some challenges.

It is my turn to watch our toddler so Phil can sleep. I try to keep it on course, but the sails flap and carry on until I have no control anymore. Yacht daddy hears all the commotion and gets up to set the sails yet again, and to steer us back on course before we do a complete circle.

I have become one of those mothers who can't control her child and needs the father to step in.

When Phil gets back to sleep, I calculate how long it will take us to get to our next scheduled stop, Waiheke Island.

We are doing five knots. At this speed, we should arrive in daylight at 6 pm. That would be nice, but now I am more experienced, I know it will not be that simple. We might;

- Need to change the sails – add 30 minutes for each change
- Need to tack away because of an oncoming wind – add at least 1 hour
- Lose speed and spend most of the trip at 3-4 knots – add 2 hours

- Need to change another fan belt – add another 30 minutes

We will probably get there about 10 pm. In the dark as usual.

The sea is not too bad today. A few wobbly bits, but the wind is slowing and waves are slight. A family of birds drifts by, floating in the ocean like bobbing bath ducks. A freighter goes past, towed by a tug boat.

It is relaxing. I have time to think in a way that I rarely do on land. At home there is always something to do or somewhere to be.

Here I can let my mind wander.

The best parts of the trip so far?

- Sunbathing on deck, cheese and crackers in hand as we watched White Island get slowly closer
- Dolphins playing under our bowsprit
- Moonlight dancing a trail across the sea to our boat
- Wandering around historic Waitangi and Russell
- The sunset while we ate seafood chowder in Tauranga

The worst parts?

- Seasickness that first day.
- Fighting to stay upright in rough seas
- Being tired and trying to run into unfamiliar ports at night

The most dramatic?

- Nearly running into a cliff
- Trying to tow another boat by their anchor
- An orange moon rising over rocks in the ocean
- The fast run into the Bay of Islands, and waves breaking over our roof.

All in all, I reckon the pluses outnumber the minuses and I have had a fabulous time.

While Phil sleeps, I watch the same headland get closer at the speed of glue drying. I eat a muesli bar, and chocolate, and liquorice, and am glad we provisioned the boat so well.

I planned fourteen breakfasts, fourteen lunches, and fourteen dinners. I also bought a bucket load of snacks for the times we couldn't face cooking even an instant dinner. At each stop, we have replenished the chocolate, lollies, and the chicken chippies. The basics really.

It has been almost three weeks since we set off, and with sea-sickness, meals on shore, and totally unsuitable meals of chicken chippies and chocolate, we still have meals left. The challenge now is to finish everything so there is no waste.

When Phil gets up, we are almost at the headland. It is my turn to sleep again and I sleep one and a half hours. When I wake up, we have made it to the headland. At least it looks the same, but it is another one entirely. Phil has been running the engine with both sails up and it has been worth it. We have made great progress. I am feeling pretty good, so I make us some steak casserole for lunch and put some fizzy vitamins in two bottles of water.

As I open my fizzy water, it sprays out so that I catch half of it on my shirt, and the rest falls to the floor with a splash. Phil looks around to see where the ocean has come in and finds me covered in red drink and looking sheepish.

He suggests a shower. The boat is rocking wildly and I would rather not, but Phil reminds me that the engine has been going and the water will be hot. I should take the chance while I can.

Right now, Manuka thinks she is a race yacht and is heeled over to the left. Everything is whirring as if we are doing a hundred, but she is only doing just over four knots. She is also rolling as usual, and only hits perpendicular when she rolls badly to the right.

I am sure this is going to be a three-bruise shower, but in the end my previous experience helps. I come out with no new bruises and just a few painful bumps on the current ones.

Two hours later, we can see skyscrapers and port cranes. I also recognise the familiar cone shape of Rangitoto Island. We are nearing Auckland city.

Small boats start crossing our path or overtaking us with surprising speed. We are the elephant of the boat world. Slow and ponderous, but I console myself that in a collision, our sixteen-ton steel boat would turn their puny fibreglass boats into microchips.

Since we started, I have spent hours like this, just relaxed and looking at ocean, and land, and sky. Hours just thinking, or pondering.

I used to have endless lists of jobs and obligations when my six sons were small. Then I worked full-time as a manager of child care centres. That was quite stressful at times.

I wonder how I would cope with appointments, deadlines, and timetables now. Especially after these two weeks of taking all morning to dress, or make and eat breakfast. The other day, I spent all afternoon watching a fishing boat go by.

Being on a yacht, has forced me to slow down and be patient in a way that maybe my ancestors might have had to when Monday was washday.

All day.

I imagine that when washing was done on a washboard, or in an old metal boiler, there was no point trying to hurry it or expecting to get much else done that day.

Taking things slow has been hard to get used to, but it has also been very rewarding. Time to think, is quite a luxury and I am grateful for it.

Now we are close to Auckland City, I call my sister. I invite her to come and visit our yacht, but it will be a shame to shatter the illusion. I have told her it is basic. I tell her it is like a caravan on water. But yachts are the toys of millionaires and playboys. They have a certain rich image that our yacht does not live up to.

It is well-made, sound, and will look a million dollars (or part thereof) when it is done up, but for now it is still grubby enough that I prefer to wear shoes inside, and I prefer not to touch some of the surfaces. Phil is keen to restore it when we get to Brisbane, but we haven't done much to make it look pretty in the three years we have owned it. All our time so far has been spent on maintenance and repairs.

I hope my sister doesn't get sick after she visits. Or stumble over the moving carpet. Or fall over one of the many other trip hazards. Or bump her head on one of the many protrusions. I hope she doesn't open the bathroom cupboard, at least not without a gas mask.

When we reach our destination, it is still daylight. Not only that, but it is only 6 pm and the shops will be open. We park well away from the shore and the only two other boats here and Phil lowers the anchor carefully by hand.

We have chosen this bay, because my GPS said there was a fish and chip shop here. Phil blows up the boat while I go online to check we have not exploded our credit card, then we head into shore.

There are small frothy waves close in to shore and we surf in on one of the bigger ones. Phil and I jump out and we are heading up the beach with our boat before any following waves can get us, feeling pretty proud of ourselves.

Half an hour later, we are back at the boat with a bag of fish and chips in one hand, and another bag with fizzy drinks, chippies, and chocolate in the other. We also have a fish cake and boar sausage. We have only been at sea a short time but every shore visit seems like a chance to buy up large.

Along with the greasy and sugary stuff, I ordered a small salad, but halfway back, I notice that the shop forgot to give it to us. I am prepared to let it go, but Phil kindly goes all the way back to get it for me while I wait.

Back at the shore, we carry everything down to the boat and the fun begins. I jump in the front while Phil pushes us out.

Then a wave pushes us back. He tries again. Another wave pushes us back. Phil is up to his waist in the water and wet to his shoulders. He gives a bigger push and jumps in. A wave crashes over the front of the boat. He tries to start the engine and it takes two goes, giving the surf enough time to swamp us a few more times.

I sit in the front with two shopping bags held over my head and laughing like demented kookaburra. It is the funniest thing. We are stuck in the frothy zone, when a few yards away the sea rolls gently entirely without waves.

Finally, the engine kicks in and we are away, through the last of the spray. Both sopping wet and both laughing fit to burst something important. We climb dripping and still sniggering into the boat.

Rather than turn the engine on and wait for it to heat up water for a shower, we boil some water and have bucket baths before enjoying our still warm and barely wet fish and chips. It is possible they are a little saltier than when we got them, but they are delicious, even the boar sausage and fishcake. The salad sits untouched.

Minutes later, Phil is asleep. I take out my contact lenses and put them in the slightly wonky inner part of my melted lenses case. I soak them in a plastic lunch box filled with water, hoping neither of us forget they are there are make hot drinks with little round plastic disks in them.

Now we are in a bay, I am confident of a good night's sleep, but it doesn't work out that way. It is quite windy where we are, but the motion is regular, as if we are on a porch swing and I find it soothing. It is our anchor alarm that wakes us up three times like another restless child.

'I can't see the sky. My GPS is not working. You have moved two feet to the left. You have changed direction.' None of it is helpful.

With that and a tummy full of fat and grease, I have a less than restful night yet again.

# Harbour Cruising

We couldn't finish all our fish and chips last night, so I heat them up for breakfast along with eggs that Phil calls 'Road Crash eggs'.

They start off in one piece but with the rocking of the boat and the difficulty of breaking the eggs on a moving surface, they don't stay that way. At least today one of the yolks is still intact.

Over our meal, Phil checks the weather report.

According to the New Zealand weather service, the cyclone has devastated Vanuatu and killed eleven people, and in a few days, it will be coming here.

We decide to head into port early. This morning we will explore this part of Waiheke Island, then this afternoon we will head out to a bay on the other side which will be more sheltered. The next day, we will run away and head for the safety of the marina.

We head into the beach again in Mini Manuka, trying to choose a quieter part of the bay than we did yesterday and wash up on shore without too much problem. We are both damp, but Phil has brought a change of shorts and goes to get changed. I don't have a change and just hope that my black shorts don't show the water.

We are in the beautiful Onepoto Bay. It is a curved sandy beach with rocks jutting into the middle area, a hill and cliffs to the left, covered with homes, and a hill to the right with a few mansion-like homes overlooking the bay. Above and parallel to the beach, a tourist area with fancy shops and prices to match. There are plenty of people in beach clothes but I don't see anyone else in wet shorts.

As we stroll along the road with no particular place to go, pondering whether to get a second ice cream or not, I notice the other tourists are overtaking us. Some of them seemed to be almost running along the footpath.

How things have changed. I used to be the one rushing and pushing to get somewhere. At one stage, I was only one more speeding ticket away from losing my licence. Now everyone is acting as if I am a speed bump on the footpath.

It makes me realise how much we have slowed down. Neither of us is in a hurry to stop sailing and we really don't want to go home. The only thing I am looking forward to is perhaps a little more sleep. After spending so many nights watching Phil adjust and readjust the sails and listening to him turn the motor on and off, or getting up to check the shrill anchor alarms useless messages, it will be nice to sleep through the night.

Other than that, this trip has given us a good taste of what it will be like to be retired. We both love it.

At the shops, I get a second ice cream. How could I not? They have salted caramel with white chocolate, cherry ripple with almond, and a muted green pistachio, just to name the three flavours that I got. I share it with Phil but still eat far too much.

We decide not to walk too far. We will sail to a beach on the other side of the island instead.

Phil puts his wet pants back on for the boat ride home and while I wait, I walk into the water to cool down. I figure I am going to get wet anyway, so I might as well start now. Phil takes long enough that as the waves get higher, I stop trying to keep my hands and shoulders dry and start diving into the waves, wondering why I didn't choose to swim earlier.

When Phil comes, I feel good. We are both already wet and I am prepared. I have been watching the waves and I notice there are several big waves and then it goes quiet. We can try to time it right. What can go wrong?

I walk further into the waves so Phil doesn't have to push me out so far. Then in my unmistakable graceful way, I dive into the boat and flounder around like a beached whale until I am in a sitting position.

There are waves coming over the front again but I don't care because I'm already wet and everything else is in a dry bag. Then Phil jumps in and leaves most of his pants behind. He is leaning over the boat with his pants around his knees and his bare bottom up to the sky.

As he falls into the boat and pulls himself together, we wonder how many people are watching from the shore. For the second time I am giggling like a school girl. I wonder if a video of Phil's bare bottom will turn up on one of those video collections of embarrassing moments. In this age of camera phones in every pocket, it is possible. If it does, I just hope we never know.

When we are back in the yacht, and clean and dry, we set sail for a bay on the other side of the island.

As we travel, I eat the apple and orange that I bought on the island along with the junk food, and we both listen to the marine radio emergency station.

A vessel is taking on water. They have one adult and two children with life jackets. Can anyone help?

By the time we work out where we think the vessel is situated, and how far it is from us, the vessel is now reported to be a dinghy.

By the time we have finished speculating on which parent has the children and how much trouble they are going to be in with the other parent, the vessel is safely ashore and the crisis is over.

After two weeks of almost no chatter over the marine radio, it is positively crackling with interesting news.

Because we are near New Zealand's biggest city and a very popular place for water sports, there are hundreds, maybe thousands of other people out on the water near here and some of them are having trouble. Yesterday, we heard several emergency calls including a jet ski stranded without power in a boat lane and a boat that was taking on water after running into rocks. It makes me feel good to know that none of our own emergencies have needed the help of the marine rescue ... so far.

It is only seven nautical miles to the next bay and we are not in a hurry. Phil puts up the sail and for the very first time on the trip, we have the wind behind us. Sailing with the wind is a completely different feeling. I can see from the GPS that we are moving but because we are at the same speed as the wind, there is no apparent wind, and we are running quite smoothly. It is almost like floating instead of sailing.

I don't have to put on a crash helmet to go down below. I can walk about the boat freely and the kitchen stuff is not sliding across the counter. I can write, or read, or do any of the usual things I can do on land. I am loving this kind of sailing.

It doesn't last.

As we round the second bay, Phil gets an update on the weather. The cyclone is going to be here earlier than we thought. After some discussion, we sadly steer away from the island and its gorgeous enticing bays, and begin our trip into the Auckland harbour and towards our safe berth.

We are now running against the wind again and the boat is jumping about a bit, but Phil decides now is a good time to make the boat shorter. The marina berth we are going into is forty feet long and we are forty-two feet. There is a wooden box that protrudes from the back of the yacht in case we want to attach an outboard motor to our giant sixteen-ton boat. We think we can live without that.

Phil stops the boat and we float around in the middle of a great space of ocean between the islands to do some work.

While Phil continues to pull the boat apart, I decide it is a good time to catch a few more fish. I have the yellow rubbery thing on the line but no other bait. After my last success, I don't think it will matter.

I tie the line around the mast so I won't get dragged in by a huge fish. The water is a lot deeper here and I am not sure what kinds of fish might be below.

Apparently, there are no fish below, at least none that want to bite my yellow rubbery thing. I am most disappointed as now I have sullied my record as a master fisherman.

Phil has been leaning over the back to undo something but now he needs help. He asks me to lean over the back and stop the bolts turning while he contorts himself into part of the hold, to undo them from the other side.

I tie off the fishing line to a mast and head over.

'Are you ready?' he says.

'I am just waiting for a ferry to pass,' I reply, not keen to wave my bottom in the air with an audience. We checked the map, and we are not in the ferry channel, but naturally, we seem to be where the ferries want to be. Several ferries have already passed quite close, as they travel back and forth to the island we have just come from.

By the time we are done, we have drifted closer to the official ferry channel and I would be glad to get going, but first we have to pack up our Mini Manuka. It isn't too hard to get the air out of it and stuff it back into its barely big enough bag. The hardest part is getting it across the deck.

There are plenty of ropes laying across our decks at trip level, but I have also added an almost invisible layer of fishing line booby traps.

It takes a few minutes to untangle the fishing line from all around the deck and under Phil's ropes. There has not been a single nibble from any fish, big or small. I wonder if I would have had more success if I had used another old piece of tofu.

As we get closer to Auckland harbour, I realise it is most likely New Zealand's busiest. When I look at the chart here, it looks as if someone has gone crazy with red and green markers. There are port and starboard markers all over the place, as well as shore lights, shipping lanes, ferry lanes, marina entrances, side channels, and miscellaneous buoys.

As we get closer to the city, small motor boats whiz past, ferries zoom by, and even other yachts gradually close in and pass us. It is a week night, so I would have thought it would be quieter, but then lots of other people may be heading in to avoid the coming cyclone.

On our right is Rangitoto Island. It is still the same low flat volcano shape that it was from the other side. On our left are some of the expensive homes that line the shore and spill up the low hill sides. Ahead on our left is the city. It looks quite compact from here, and dominated by the Sky tower with its tall spire topped with a ball.

It is pretty here but I am not enjoying it as much as usual. This is the end of our sailing trip. We will soon be in the marina and packing up. The coming cyclone has cut our fun short and I really don't want it to end.

It takes almost two hours to get as far as the city and we still have a few more hours to go. At least we should be well protected from the weather back here. The map shows our marina at the end of a long narrow curved channel, well away from the main harbour. Phil suggests we will probably be able to hear the banjos up there.

After we sail under the huge steel arches of the harbour bridge, there seem to be a few less boats. Many of them have sailed into the three marinas that are closer to the city.

Phil decides now would be a good time to take apart some more of the boat. He wants to remove the great heavy wooden and steel bowsprit that sticks out the front and holds the foremost sail.

He starts pulling things apart while I steer and try to avoid the fisherman in their low aluminium dinghies that are very hard to see. Especially with Phil at the front. We are running the engine at higher than usual revs because we want to be in the marina before dark.

Suddenly I smell burning. I slow the engine down. Phil comes back to see why I have slowed and tells me to stop the engine.

He goes below, and we have torn another fan belt into shreds. It means another belt change and Phil doesn't have much time. We are quite close to shore and have no power.

As he goes below, I watch carefully and realise that we are drifting quite fast. Within minutes we will be up close and personal with the only yacht anchored for miles. It just happens to be right here, between us and the shore.

Phil charges back up, starts the engine and moves us quickly over to another spot. He heads below again while I watch us drift closer to a group of fishermen in small boat. They don't seem impressed to have us hovering so close. Then I hear a cry.

'What happened?' I say.

'Nothing,' he replies. 'I just burned myself.'

That is one of the things that first attracted me to Phil. He is amazingly calm under pressure.

I go back to watching the fishermen who are pretending not to notice us, and see that the current is now taking us away from the fishermen and back towards the shore and the lone yacht. Just as if we are magnetised to each other.

Phil comes back up. He is sporting a nice red burn across his forearm and complaining about the way the engine is so badly laid out, but he has managed the change.

'Do we have any more fan belts?' I ask.

'Plenty,' he says. 'The previous owner must have decided it was easier to have a dozen spare fanbelts than to fix the motor.'

We set off at lower revs and hope we can still make it into the marina before dark. We are not too far away now.

'Is that our marina?' Phil asks pointing across the bay.

'No,' I say confidently. The sun is setting right in front of us and I can't even see what he is pointing at, but our marina is up a long and curved channel. I am sure we can't possibly see it from here.

An hour later, we pull into that very marina. It turns out our 'long curved channel' is only a line on our map, and a few red and green beacons on the water. The map has brought us all the way around the harbour to a point that was just across from us.

When we see the area at low tide the next day, we are glad we followed the map. There are mangrove trees and muddy shoals all across the bay. If we had sailed directly to the marina, we would have got caught in submerged branches or beached on shallow sand shoals.

When we sail into the marina and tie up to our new berth, a security officer is there to meet us and show us around. We check out the showers and laundry, and I get a new book to read from the pile on a table. We made it just before dark and we are ready to relax. Or so we think.

We have an early night but below us there is a strange noise that keeps us awake.

At first it sounds like a small fire of crackling twigs. Then we wonder if maybe it is our steel boat gradually falling apart. It has a vaguely electrical sound as if bits of paint and metal are popping off. Phil suggests I look it up on google.

I find someone on Google who has heard a sound under their boat that sounds like milk on rice crispies.

'That's what it sounds like,' Phil says, and I agree.

'It's snapping shrimp,' I tell him. 'They snap their claws in such a way that the air pops and makes that distinctive sound.'

Now that we know our boat is not falling apart, we can relax and go to sleep. And we can also expect be secure and safe here from the coming storm.

# Windy in Town

The next day it is halfway through the afternoon and all we have done is rest. I woke up first and started writing. Phil woke up later with a headache. He went for a walk and came back with some eggs and cheese. I made an omelette and now he has gone back to sleep. Hardly an adventurous day, but a nice quiet interlude.

The sky today is silver with rounded grey and white clouds, in great puffs overhead. There was some wind last night but this morning it has definitely got worse. Every little breeze in a marina can sound like a gale as it makes a whooshing sound through so many sails and ropes, but I think this is the storm.

I am so glad we came here yesterday and not today. Phil had one of his 'feelings' that sent us into the marina early and he has never been wrong yet.

If this is it, we are lucky. From the radio, we learn that the storm hit Vanuatu at 150 mph and left 75,000 people without a home. There were only eleven confirmed deaths but that is because the country is experienced with cyclones and the islanders took measures to keep themselves safe.

Where we are, there are several rows of boats between us and the harbour. Then there is a small rock wall and a large expanse of protected water between us and the ocean. I can hear wind but not feel it. I don't know if it is 150 mph or not but I can't help thinking about the picture in the Tauranga Marina of yachts all piled up on one another after a cyclone in a North Australian marina. We are quite far inland and I think we are safe.

By 7 pm, Phil has gone to bed and is sleeping soundly. After what we have been through for the last three weeks, he has a lot to recover from. Loss of sleep, worry, mechanical failures, bad weather, and boat damage. It has been an amazing adventure. Now there is nothing to do today but sleep, and write, and read the Stephen King thriller that I found in the yacht club laundry last night.

Later, I will take up some rubbish and check out the fresh food options. Tomorrow, I will do washing and maybe book our flights home. Such is the life of a yachty. Some days are all stormy seas and hard work. Some days are all dolphins and beautiful shores. Other days are just quiet in between days. But that is part of the adventure. The uncertainty and the unexpected.

As the day wears on, it rains and the wind continues to howl. It is a great day for writing and staying inside, so we do. We have one little trip to the café where Phil gets a late breakfast and I get a smoothie. During a small lull in the weather, we start a small excursion by walking up the hill near the marina, but the rain starts again so we don't get far.

I feel like fish chowder, so I make a lovely thick seafood flavoured chowder that has absolutely no seafood in it. I thought we would catch so many fish, we would get sick of eating it plain so I bought some crumbs for crumbed fish, instant mashed potato for fish pie, and coconut cream and seafood soup powder for a fish chowder. We haven't used any of it.

I use the last of the canned chicken for my 'seafood chowder', and while I don't see this recipe winning any culinary awards or becoming the next YouTube sensation, I quite like it. Phil says he likes it too, but then he loves me and would say that.

Sunday is a slow and relaxing day and a much-needed chance to rest and recover. One a few more days to go and then we leave for home.

# Cleaning Up and Packing Up

Because our yacht is not much bigger than your average caravan, there is limited space and the area needs constant tidying to keep things in order. That is what we are doing today. Sorting and tidying. Phil has pulled all the 'stuff' out of the floor storage areas and it litters our main cabin floor. He plans to clean the inside of the hull and wash off the salt.

I collect our washing and take it down to the marina laundry. We have a lot of washing. There are damp clothes from our adventure in Mini Manuka as well as hand-washing I did a few days ago in Waitangi that has not dried. There is also our quilt. When I woke up this morning it had a large wet patch.

The canvas cover that I stitched so carefully in Gisborne, came apart during the trip along with almost every other zip on the cover and the wind has blown rain through the gaps. It also dripped from our bedroom ceiling through a tiny unsealed crack. When I woke up the quilt top was wet. At least we were dry underneath.

Phil takes the canvas to be repaired at a business in the marina compound and I get our plane tickets home. This yacht is costing us money, right up to the last.

My sister calls again. She lives quite close so we arrange that she will come by for lunch tomorrow. She says she is really looking forward to seeing our yacht. I am not so excited. It has never looked worse. Things are all over the deck while Phil cleans the hold. The carpet is still a trip hazard and looks as if it was made for another boat. There are rusty steel pipes tied to the handrail, and rust stains sliding down the hull. It looks like our hull is in the process of melting.

To make it even worse, Phil had a little accident in the boat earlier. He was using the hose to clean inside the hull, when the end came off and the water sprayed all over. He took the carpet out to air but we can't leave it out any more in case it rains. Tomorrow it will probably still smell of wet carpet.

'What if she looks in the bathroom cupboard?' I ask Phil. 'It smells as if someone died in there.'

Phil suggests I borrow another yacht to show her. I am seriously tempted; I just don't know anyone here. He also offers to distract her just before she arrives at our yacht by setting fire to his pants and running down the other row of berths. I would like to see that but regretfully decline

I joke about it but I really don't mind too much. I have no desire to be envied. I am having fun and I know she has been having fun too. We are at a good age and stage in life. Her man likes horse racing, and mine likes yachts. Right now, I think that both of us are in a great place with very supportive partners. There is no need to try and impress her.

We have a lovely visit amongst the mass of boat bits. When she leaves, she takes home a small bag of leftover food that will not last until we visit again.

Life is good.

It has been a difficult journey at times, but not life threatening. There were no mid-sea rescues. No sliding down fifty-foot waves. No sign of a Kraken, not even a single snake-like tentacle.

Our crusty old lifesaving ring is still dry and untested and the emergency number in our satellite phone has not been needed. Our life jackets didn't even get wet.

We also didn't get the yacht home.

As is so often in life, the journey has been more important than the destination. This has been one of those times when we didn't achieve our goals, but we got something even better, a few weeks of adventure, and a safe return home.

Every day has been a lesson in patience and flexibility. We have had to rely on the wind and weather to get us places. We have learned to cope with problems that have no easy solution. We took moments as they came and worked with whatever the day delivered.

Most of our modern world is all about speed and instant gratification. Faster microwaves, instant dinners, take-outs at drive-through windows and jobs that have deadlines and quotas. Sailing has forced me to slow down.

To our surprise, both of us have also lost a little weight despite eating too much junk food. Perhaps it is because we have been active and used muscles that have been in hibernation for too long. Perhaps it is because even just sitting down in a moving yacht is hard work. I have been stretched well beyond my comfort zone and come out feeling better about myself.

I am glad that this time we had the option of stopping along the way because we sure needed it, but it has been a great introduction to sailing and has fulfilled my requirements for a wonderful adventure. It was never boring.

This has been the adventure of a lifetime and it has left me with a taste for more sailing and more adventure ... and that can only be a good thing.

# Epilogue – Welcome Home

One year after our big trip around the North-East coast of New Zealand, I stood at the end of a Brisbane wharf watching anxiously downstream.

After an hour of patient waiting, an indistinct shape riding low in the water finally hove into view. It approached interminably slowly. First a slim line of hull topped with two erect masts, then a cabin with faint dark shapes on board that gradually turned into three tired looking sailors, with exhausted but triumphant faces. If I had any doubt about which boat it was, the steady pounding of a worn-out tractor engine coming from inside, was all too familiar.

They had some trouble seeing us through the boats already tied up in the busy marina, but finally aimed for the large welcome home banner I had tied on to the wrong side of the customs metal fence. After ten days at sea, my husband, assisted by his brother and brother-in-law, had completed the Tasman crossing.

It was a bittersweet moment. I was thrilled that they had made it back safe, but sad that I had not been with them. I had expected to be part of the great ocean adventure that brought our yacht home to Australia, but I was needed at home. Instead of travelling with me, a wife with two weeks sailing experience who felt more like 'cargo than crew', Phil had crossed the Tasman Sea with a brother and brother-in-law who between them had - even less experience. For both of them, it was their first ever sailing trip, but it was the right decision. They were more mechanically helpful, and stayed awake long enough to help on those long dark mid-ocean nights.

The trip took ten days from Opua, New Zealand to Brisbane, Australia. For the most part, it was plain sailing, with large comfortable ocean swells and favourable winds that blew them home. It must have been magic, looking out across a vast expanse of ocean and feeling so insignificant.

Then, on day seven, there was a full on gale. For almost two days, they had torrential rain and over 35 knot winds. Water sprayed over the boat and into the cabin making a small well of sloppy six-inch-deep water. A tub of butter floated all around the cabin, spreading its oily cheer everywhere. On those days, there was a lot of praying both on board and at my end. I knew from personal experience that the boat would manage wild weather, but I did worry about the comfort and welfare of the crew. On one memorable night, Phil called to say that they were off to bed to sleep out the storm – at 6pm.

Although he called twice a day, every call was brief because they were made on an excessively expensive satellite phone. We spent that minute reporting his co-ordinates and swapping weather updates, and not much more. Phil and I normally talk about everything and I had really missed our time together.

As Phil steered the yacht into the berth, and his brothers helped tie up the boat, I stood behind the barrier and hopped from foot to foot, looking forward to hearing more about the trip and impatient for that first warm hug.

My husband, jumped off onto the wharf and stood behind the metal customs fence, smiling awkwardly. Then he said his first welcoming words on Australian soil.

'I broke your computer'.

Not the greeting I was expecting.

Then, because we were still separated by the customs barrier, he said 'and can you go pay the customs bill?'

Welcome back Phil. I considered leaving him there.

A customs officer arrived soon after, and checked all over the boat - poking into every crevice and orifice of the yacht, looking for contraband and not finding it. No drugs, no cigarettes and no illegal immigrants hiding under the seats.

I sat on a concrete wall next to the wharf gate and waited while my bottom became increasingly numb. It took over an hour before he left the boat, dragging a large black sack containing their empty cans, bottles, and food packets.

With his departure, the boys had officially cleared customs and could pass the barrier. I was able to welcome back my husband with a warm hug and a cool accusation. 'You broke my computer? Why?'

He said an unexpected rough patch had thrown a few wild and well-aimed waves into the boat and up over the navigation table. Luckily, it had happened that last morning, so they only had to rely on their phones for navigation for just a few hours. A waterproof computer bag is now on my list of must-haves for the next trip.

The boys stayed that night in the marina and then the next afternoon, Phil and I sailed Manuka across the smooth, sandy-bottomed stretch of protected water that is Moreton Bay. The boat ran effortlessly with the wind while Phil and I stood on deck, watching the sun set over the Redcliffe Peninsular and sipping cool drinks. This was a whole new experience for me. Sailing without bouncing. Sailing without a throbbing engine. Sailing without bruises.

Sailing in this part of Australia *is* more like the dictionary definition of sailing. It is floating and gliding smoothly. I look forward to more of this kind of sailing. There are the famous Whitsundays to explore, with their calm waters, and smooth white sand, like icing around a thousand green island cakes.

There is the Great Barrier Reef, a world-wide wonder, with its sapphire waters and vibrant landscape of multi-faceted coral and rainbow hued fish. We will probably see whales, and rays, and maybe even dugongs, the shy sea cow that hides in the waters of our local bay.

There are many more adventures to come, but I wouldn't change my first sailing trip for anything. It was wild, and adventurous, and a journey I will never forget. It made me feel alive in a way that I have not experienced often in my usually sedate and careful life. There is real merit in being uncomfortable sometimes; in taking a few risks, and doing something so difficult that everything else changes, including the way you feel about yourself and your abilities.

Every day was a lesson in patience and flexibility. We had to rely on the wind and weather (and a cantankerous old engine) to get us places. We learned to cope with problems that had no easy solution. We took moments as they came and worked with whatever the day delivered. I was stretched well beyond my comfort zone, but I loved it and learned so much. I still have trouble with some sailing terms but I now know my Starboard from my Port, and a boom from a gib. I know some of the ships navigation and radar systems and I will never forget what a davit is.

Phil has accomplished a long-held dream, and is preparing for the next; a year living on the boat while we travel Australia, maybe even the Pacific.

We had the adventure of a lifetime and that can only be a good thing

May all your travel dreams come true, and all your trials make you stronger. Best wishes. *Nikki*

# Nikki's other travel books

## Housesitting in Australia
*Big Adventures on a Tiny Budget*

HouseSitting
in
Australia

Big Adventures on a Tiny Budget
*Nikki Ah Wong*

On the brink of turning fifty, Nikki's life spirals into chaos. Her marriage crumbles, her health deteriorates, and her six children start forging their own paths. Then a harrowing run in with an online predator leads to her losing her corporate job.

Nikki decides to sell everything and move to sunny Brisbane, Australia, where she embarks on a journey of self-discovery and reinvention. First, she joins a health retreat to support those battling addiction. When that falls through, she stumbles upon a new passion: house-sitting.

Embracing the nomadic lifestyle, Nikki cares for others' homes and pets while exploring. She takes up motorbike riding, rallies around Tasmania, and learns to live on a shoestring budget. By year's end, she emerges transformed.

This inspiring memoir not only chronicles Nikki's journey of growth and self-discovery but also serves as a valuable guide for aspiring house sitters. Learn the ins and outs of house-sitting, from finding opportunities to crafting successful applications.

Whether you're considering house-sitting or contemplating a life change, let Nikki's story motivate and inspire you to embrace the possibilities.

# A Middle-Aged Princess in Tramping Boots

*Adventures in Life, Love, and House Sitting*

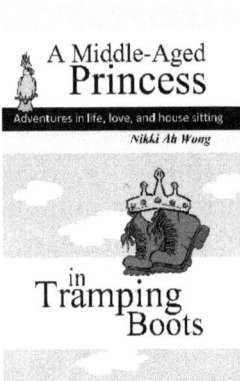

If you are looking for an inspiring story about a midlife awakening to adventure then you will love this book. Nikki takes us inside everything from a home in a million-dollar gated community, to the back of a car in a McDonalds car park.

In this, her second year, she also takes us to Outback New South Wales and over to New Zealand to stay on a run-down yacht. She explores the ocean, both from above and below and shares her often humorous experiences with online dating. Also included is an appendix of useful resources and tips for anyone interested in finding, applying for, and succeeding at, house sits.

## Junk Mail Princess

*Adventures in Life, Love, Renovation, and Junk Mail*

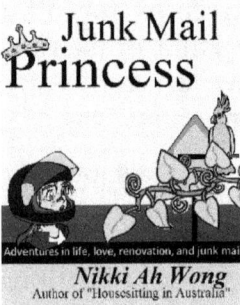

After two years living in other people's homes, Nikki marries the man of her dreams and buys the home of no one's dreams. It is filthy, stinky, and there is a working toilet in the middle of the downstairs floor.

Then she accepts a job delivering junk mail and the fun really starts. Will Nikki survive the attack poodles and the junk mail haters to make her delivery to every home in Brisbane? Will the house from hell turn into a palace fit for a Princess? Find out in Junk Mail Princess.

# The House Sitters Companion
*Journal and Planner*

The essential resource for house sitters, with handy calendars, note pages, and lists to help you plan and record your house-sitting experiences

*All books are available at Amazon.com and other major booksellers*

You can also follow Nikki on her blog at

## www.travellerinoz.blogspot.com

If you have a minute, please consider leaving a review on your favourite book site. Good reviews are treasured by hard-working authors and they help other readers find good books to read.

# Acknowledgements

This is my fourth book about adventures and loving life and as always, I have many people to thank.

Firstly Phil. As you can tell from the story, he is that rare and unusual man who will do whatever is needed without complaint. He made this adventure happen, and kept it going, even when my only contribution was lie in my bunk and try not to be sick. Without him, there would have been no sailing, and nothing to write about.

I am grateful for my writer friends who offered suggestions and made some important corrections to facts and dates. I would particularly like to mention Suzi Tooke. I am grateful for your corrections to the early draft. Since then, I have added a lot more material, so I apologise if I have also added back errors.

Breanda Cross. Thank you for caring enough to find me readers who had been sailing. Having them read early drafts provided much helpful feedback.

To the Queensland Coast Guard service, a big thank you. Having them watching over our journey and knowing they would follow up if we went missing was reassuring. They run a crucial and supportive service for those of us out sailing, and most are volunteers who give up their free time to keep us safe.

Lastly, thank you to you, my reader. I hope you enjoyed the story and found something to inspire you.

# About the Author

Nikki Lentfer (Previously published as Nikki Ah Wong) is the mother of six sons and a grandmother. A few years ago, she was a well-paid manager for a national childcare organization in New Zealand and managed up to 120 people. After living for two years with no fixed income, no fixed address and moving from home to home as a house sitter, she has settled down on two acres in Brisbane.

Nikki describes herself as an explorer and a wonder aficionado. She has taught workshops on topics that range from getting organized, to digital scrapbooking, to writing for the media. She has promoted and managed a range of community events from Children's Day activities to a week of family events.

Nikki has a diploma in Freelance Journalism, and a diploma in Internet Marketing and E-Commerce. She was a part time Public Affairs and Media Specialist for almost 20 years and has had many articles published in magazines and newspapers.